My First Scene Book
Acting Out, Acting Up, Acting Right

My First WITHDRAWN Scene Book

Acting Out, Acting Up, Acting Right

51 One-Minute Scenes for Young Children

by Kristen Dabrowski

MY FIRST ACTING SERIES: VOLUME 4

A SMITH AND KRAUS BOOK • HANOVER, NEW HAMPSHIRE

A Smith and Kraus Book
Published by Smith and Kraus, Inc.
177 Lyme Road, Hanover, NH 03755
www.SmithandKraus.com

First Edition: October 2008
Manufactured in the United States of America
9 8 7 6 5 4 3 2 1

ISBN-13: 978-1-57525-603-0 / ISBN-10 1-57525-603-7
Library of Congress Control Number: 2008927865

To Mrs. Anderson, Mrs. Challener, and
Mrs. Paxton, my K–2 teachers,
who found ways to make learning easy!

Contents

Foreword   xi

Acting Lessons   xiv

Part 1: GROSS!   1

Dinner Time   2

The Kiss   6

Lisa's Ponytail   11

Food Fight   15

Coffee Talk   20

Mine, Not Yours   25

No Manners   30

Part 2: SCARY!   35

Suddenly Sick   36

Homework?   40

No More!   45

Too Shy   50

No Nurses!   56

Lost   61

Whoops!   67

The Deep End   73

Part 3: SNEAKY!   79

The Pen   80
Trouble Maker   84
The Test   89
Poly-Poly Roland   93
Bedtime   98

PART 4: NO FAIR!   103

The Cat's Best Friend   104
Rajah's Last Day   109
Two Steps Ahead   114
Paint Hog   119
Gorilla My Dreams   123
The Movie   127
Miss Rockin' Robots   132
Socks for Christmas   137

Part 5: MEAN!   143

The Game   144
Baby Sister   149
Turkey Face   154
Howdy, Partner   159
Back Off, Brandy   163
Candy Day   168
Not Invited   175

Part 6: ANNOYING!   **181**

A Sticky Situation   182

Summer Vacation   187

Show Off   193

Inside Voice   198

Jack's Got the Blues   203

It's My Party   207

Baby Blob   212

Part 7: CONFUSING!   **217**

Grandma's Here   218

You're It   223

Smarty Ants   227

Timmy's Story   232

Joselyn Takes Over the Universe   237

Addy Knows the Answer   243

Mother's Day   247

Poor Ben   254

Happy Face   258

Foreword

Welcome to My First Acting Series! If you are not five to nine years old, PUT DOWN THIS BOOK! (OK, if you are a parent, guardian, teacher, agent, or someone's who's just interested, you are welcome, too.)

In *My First Monologue Book*, we learned about what a monologue is and how to rehearse one. That book covered basic, everyday situations for kids like not wanting to go to bed, having to eat broccoli, and making new friends. If you haven't already seen it, check it out!

Now you know how to act like a kid your age, whether that boy or girl is nice, selfish, funny, smart—or all those things! *My Second Monologue Book* stretches your acting skills and your imagination even further. You can act out many historical, famous, and imaginary characters. This means you can play adults who do different jobs and come from different parts of the world.

My Third Monologue Book challenges your imagination and your brain! In this book, you act out characters in places far and near. Plus, you have to guess where the character is—in Egypt? Chicago? Oz? This book is very interactive. See what it's like to play detective!

Finally, in this book, we get to scenes! Whoopie! *My First Scene Book* shows situations a lot of kids will recognize. These situations are tricky and sticky, though: When do you listen to the rules? When do you break the rules? What are rules for? Why should you be polite? What do you do if other people don't act nice? Discussion questions at the end of each scene help you think about what is happening and decide how you feel about the characters and situations.

Act out the characters for your family and friends! See if you can become this person with how you act and how you dress. Be creative! There's no wrong way to use this book. Dress up, have girls do boys' parts, make some of the girls into boys, write in the book, draw in the book, color the pictures—whatever you like! Feel free to ask adults and teachers for help with words you do not understand.

(Note: Parents and teachers, since these scenes are meant to be conversational, this book contains a lot of contractions and sentence fragments. It is a good opportunity to discuss what contractions are as well as the difference between formal language and conversational language. The goals of this book are primarily to sound realistic, provoke questions and opinions, create a unique acting volume, question morals and manners, and be a reading comprehension guide. Agents and managers, because the language in this book is highly conversational, it is a very good source for scenes that meet kids where they are now, developmentally.)

Next in the series will be *My Second Scene Book*. This book will have far-out scenes and imaginative people, places, and events! What is it like to live on the moon? Be a dragon? Battle a wizard? Prepare yourself for the adventure of your life as you put together all of the skills in the previous books in this series!

See how these books grow with you and your skills? Each book builds on the one before it.

- **Teachers:** Look for the *Teacher's Guide* to this series for many ideas about how to use this book in the classroom.

- **English/Drama Teachers and Parents:** There will also be a guide to acting (*My First Acting Book*) with theater games, exercises, acting techniques, and information on how to be an actor.

- **Agents:** These monologues are immediate and active, with different emotions and levels within each monologue. Great for auditions.

Enjoy and explore!

Kristen Dabrowski

Acting Lessons

1. A scene is a short play with more than one character.

2. When you are reading a scene out loud, think and talk like your character.

3. Try to understand how your character thinks and feels. This is very important! When you are an actor, you should behave just like your character.

4. Here are some examples of stage directions:

   (CARL *walks over to AUNT ROCHELLE.*)

   (MOM *exits.*)

   (PENNY *starts to smile.*)

   (ROBIN *runs away.*)

   Stage directions are things the characters do in a scene. When you are reading a scene out loud, have someone play the narrator and read all the stage directions. When you are acting out a scene, you can just act out what the stage directions say.

5. When you perform a scene in front of an audience,

make sure you speak loudly, so everyone can hear you.

6. When you perfo rm a scene in front of an audience, pay attention to the other people onstage.

7. When you perfo rm a scene in front of an audience, walk and dress like your character, too!

8. To memorize (remember without looking at the book) your lines, get a friend or a family member to say them with you over and over and over again.

9. If you are playing a character older or younger than you, think about how this might change how you think, walk, talk, and dress.

Part 1
GROSS!

What are these characters saying?
What's going on in this picture?
You decide!

DINNER TIME

Gina and Lucy have terrible table manners!

Characters
Lucy
Gina

(LUCY and GINA sit at a table.)

LUCY: Give me the butter.

GINA: Please.

LUCY: Give me the butter!

GINA: Please!

LUCY: Uh, OK, fine. Pleeeeease.

GINA: That's better.

LUCY: You're so bossy, Gina.

GINA: You're so rude, Lucy!

LUCY: I am not!

GINA: You never say please.

LUCY: So what? Please is just another stupid word. Why can't I just say, "Give me the butter"?

GINA: Because it's not polite.

LUCY: What if I say, "give me the butter" in a really nice voice?

GINA: It's still rude.

LUCY: Why? That doesn't make sense to me.

GINA: It's the rules.

LUCY: Why are there so many rules?! I hate it. Clean you room. Brush your teeth. Say please! I get so sick of being told what to do.

GINA: Why can't you just do all that stuff without complaining? What's the big deal? It's not hard to say please or brush your teeth.

LUCY: But I don't want to!

GINA: You have to!

LUCY: Why why why!

GINA: If you don't brush your teeth, they will fall out, and your breath will stink, and you'll have no friends. If you don't say please, people will think you're rude.

LUCY: But why?

GINA: I can't take it! You don't understand anything!

(GINA starts eating food with her hands, shoveling things into her mouth.)

LUCY: What are you doing?!

GINA: What's wrong?

LUCY: You're eating with your hands!

GINA: So?

LUCY: So it's disgusting!

GINA: *(Licking her fingers.)* No, it's not.

LUCY: Oh yes, it is! I'm getting sick just looking at you.

GINA: You're being rude again.

LUCY: You think I'm being rude, but you don't think you're disgusting?

GINA: No! I mean, yes! You're rude, and I'm fine.

LUCY: You're licking your fingers!

GINA: There's food on them.

LUCY: You are impossible!

GINA: Mind your own business. Just eat your soup.

LUCY: Fine.

(LUCY begins slurping her soup. At the same time, GINA burps.)

GINA/LUCY: Gross!

GINA/LUCY: You are!

Questions

1. What things do Gina and Lucy do that show poor table manners?

2. Which girl has the worst behavior? Or are they even?

3. Are there any rules that don't make sense to you?

4. What are some other things that are polite?

5. Why do people say "please" and "thank you"?

6. Are there any questions you have about table manners?

7. Which is worse: Chewing with your mouth open or spitting your food out if you don't like it?

8. What is the hardest food to eat politely and why?

9. Do you eat differently at home than you do in restaurants? Why or why not?

10. What should you say if someone serves you a food you don't like?

THE KISS

Anthony has a great time at his grammy's.
Until he has to kiss her good-bye!

Characters

Dad
Anthony
Grammy

DAD: OK, Anthony. Time to go.

ANTHONY: Grammy said I could have one more cookie.

DAD: Your grandmother spoils you!

GRAMMY: That is a grandmother's job.

(*GRAMMY gives ANTHONY a cookie.*)

ANTHONY: Is it true that you were my dad's mom?

GRAMMY: That's right, still am!

ANTHONY: So Dad was a boy once?

DAD: Of course I was! Did you think I was born all grown-up?

ANTHONY: What kind of boy was he, Grammy?

GRAMMY: A good boy . . . most of the time.

ANTHONY: Did he get in trouble?

GRAMMY: Not much, but sometimes. Would you like some milk with that?

ANTHONY: Yes, please. What did he do to get in trouble?

GRAMMY: Once he—

DAD: Don't give him any ideas, Mom!

GRAMMY: They were just boy things, like you probably do, Anthony. One time he broke a window with a baseball. He failed a class in school—

DAD: It was ballroom dancing! They made us dance with girls.

ANTHONY: Dad failed a class?! Wow.

DAD: Just once. Don't get any ideas, Anthony.

GRAMMY: Do you want anything else, dear?

ANTHONY: Another cookie?

DAD: Nope, Anthony, that's it. We gotta go home now.

ANTHONY: Aw, Dad, we were just getting to the good stuff. I want to hear about more bad things Dad did.

GRAMMY: Your father was a very good boy. Still is.

DAD: Get your coat on, Anthony.

(ANTHONY puts on his coat. DAD puts on his coat, too.)

GRAMMY: You boys come back and visit me soon, OK?

DAD: Of course we will, Mom.

(DAD hugs GRAMMY.)

DAD: Anthony, give Grammy a kiss.

ANTHONY: What?

DAD: Give Grammy a kiss.

ANTHONY: No!

DAD: What? Young man, you do what you're told.

ANTHONY: I don't wanna!

DAD: Your grammy made you lunch and baked cookies for you, and you won't give her a kiss?

ANTHONY: No, thank you.

GRAMMY: Oh, it's OK.

DAD: It is not OK! Anthony, I want you to give your grandmother a kiss right now!

ANTHONY: Ooooh, Daaaaaad . . .

DAD: Go ahead, young man.

GRAMMY: I promise I won't bite!

(ANTHONY slowly walks over to GRAMMY. GRAMMY leans over and sticks her cheek toward ANTHONY. ANTHONY slooooooowly leans in toward GRAMMY and gives her a very, very quick kiss. Afterward, he wipes his mouth.)

ANTHONY: Yech.

DAD: You stop that, young man. I'm sorry, Mom.

GRAMMY: I know Anthony loves me and my cookies. You boys be safe on the way home.

(DAD and ANTHONY exit GRAMMY's house.)

DAD: Young man, we are going to have a talk when we get home about your manners!

ANTHONY: What did I do?

Questions

1. What did Anthony do wrong?

2. How do you think Grammy feels?

3. Why is Dad mad at Anthony?

4. Should Anthony have to kiss his grandmother?

5. Is there another, better way for Anthony to get out of kissing Grammy?

6. Why do boys hate to kiss girls?

LISA'S PONYTAIL

Kevin keeps pulling Lisa's hair. Does he like her?

Characters
Kevin
Lisa
Maria

KEVIN: Lisa, you smell like poo!

LISA: No, I don't!

MARIA: Takes one to know one, Kevin.

(KEVIN pulls LISA's ponytail.)

LISA: Ow!

MARIA: Why did you do that?

KEVIN: Why not?

LISA: That hurt!

MARIA: I know why you did that.

KEVIN: Oh yeah?

MARIA: Yeah! You like Lisa.

KEVIN: I do not!

MARIA: Yes, you do.

KEVIN: No, I don't!

LISA: Why would he pull my ponytail and call me names if he likes me?

KEVIN: Yeah, why would I do that if I liked her?

MARIA: Because you're in love.

KEVIN: That doesn't make sense.

MARIA: Sure it does.

LISA: I don't get it.

MARIA: If he didn't love you, he would just go away.

LISA: Well, that's true. Why don't you just go away, Kevin, and leave me alone?

KEVIN: Maybe I will.

MARIA: See, he's still here. He wants to get your attention. That's what my mama says. Remember last year when Bobby Lee wouldn't leave me alone?

LISA: I remember.

MARIA: Well, my mama told me it's because he liked me. And she was right! One day he said he wanted to marry me.

LISA: Ew!

KEVIN: That is so gross!

MARIA: I know, but he was mean to me for a long time before that. But even though he was being mean, he really wanted to kiss me!

LISA: I would rather have a boy be mean to me than kiss me!

MARIA: I know!

LISA: Best of all would be if boys could just act nice and normal.

MARIA: My mama says it's impossible. That's how boys are.

KEVIN: I don't like Lisa. She has cooties. I don't ever want to kiss girls!

(KEVIN pulls LISA's ponytail and run away.)

MARIA: He's going to ask you to marry him soon.

LISA: I don't want to be married to Kevin! What should I do?

MARIA: Well, when Bobby Lee asked me to marry him, I asked my mama what to do. She said to tell him that I can't get married for thirty years. So I told him, and he married Marsha Dubecker.

LISA: They got married?

MARIA: Yeah. Can you believe it?

Questions

1. Do you think Kevin likes Lisa?
2. Why do boys pull girls' hair?
3. Why are boys sometimes mean to girls?
4. Why are girls sometimes mean to boys?
5. Why do some children pretend to get married?
6. What's the best way to get someone's attention?

FOOD FIGHT

Ruby does not want to eat creamed spinach!

Characters
Ruby
Dad
Myles
Kendall

(DAD, RUBY, MYLES, and KENDALL sit at a table with plates and forks.)

RUBY: Yuck. What is this?

DAD: That is creamed spinach.

RUBY: Yuck.

DAD: Just eat it.

RUBY: I don't want to.

MYLES: Just eat a little.

RUBY: No. It looks terrible.

DAD: Don't be rude. Just eat it.

KENDALL: It's not too bad. It just looks gross.

RUBY: It smells bad, too.

DAD: It does not smell bad. Stop making a fuss, Ruby.

RUBY: I really, really don't want to eat it.

MYLES: You're such a picky eater.

RUBY: So?

MYLES: So it's a pain.

KENDALL: It's not so bad. I swear, Ruby. *(Eating.)* See?

RUBY: No. I am not eating that.

DAD: Ruby, you have to try it. That's the rule. At least try it.

RUBY: Dad, I can't!

DAD: Yes, you can.

RUBY: Noooo!

MYLES: Stop complaining!

KENDALL: Just try a little. A tiny bit!

RUBY: Why is it the rule that I have to try everything. I don't like everything.

KENDALL: How do you know you don't like it? You haven't tried it.

DAD: It's just the rule. You have to try everything.

RUBY: Everything? What if I tried poison or dirt?

MYLES: You are such a pain.

DAD: You know what I mean.

RUBY: You said we have to try everything.

DAD: Enough joking around. Eat your dinner, Ruby.

RUBY: I'd rather eat toilet paper.

MYLES: You have to eat what is on your plate. There's no toilet paper on your plate.

RUBY: Why do I have to try everything?

KENDALL: So you'll be healthy. Right, Dad?

DAD: That's right.

RUBY: I am healthy.

KENDALL: Maybe you won't stay that way.

MYLES: Maybe your tongue will fall off if you don't eat spinach. Then we will finally have a quiet meal!

DAD: Just eat it, Ruby. It's good for you.

RUBY: I hate rules. They're stupid. If I tried everything, I'd have to eat shoes and cigarettes and sticks and worms—

DAD: Either you eat that spinach or I will make you eat a worm!

RUBY: You said I just have to try a little!

DAD: That's right.

(RUBY quickly touches the spinach to her lips.)

RUBY: Blech! I tried it. OK?

DAD: I guess so.

MYLES: She didn't even swallow any! You're so spoiled, Ruby.

RUBY: I am not!

MYLES: You are, too. You're such a brat.

DAD: Everyone, just eat your dinner.

KENDALL: I like spinach!

DAD: That's great, Kendall!

MYLES: You're such a goody two-shoes, Kendall!

Questions

1. Is Ruby being too picky?

2. Why do parents have rules?

3. What do you think of the rule "You have to try everything"?

4. Why is Myles calling everyone names? What do you think of Myles?

5. What foods do you hate to eat?

6. Do you have any rules at home about eating? What are they?

7. Should Ruby have eaten the spinach?

COFFEE TALK

Charlie wants to try coffee.

Characters

Charlie
Mom
Daisy
Dad

(CHARLIE, DAISY, MOM, and DAD sit at a table. MOM and DAD have coffee mugs in front of them.)

CHARLIE: Can I have some coffee, Dad?

MOM: Charlie, you're too young to have coffee.

CHARLIE: Why?

DAISY: Caffeine is bad for you.

CHARLIE: What's caffeine?

DAISY: Bad stuff in coffee.

CHARLIE: What is so bad about it?

DAD: It makes you jumpy and nervous.

CHARLIE: Then why do you drink it?

DAD: It's a grown-up thing.

CHARLIE: I hate it when you say that. Can't I just try it?

MOM: Charlie, what did I tell you?

CHARLIE: You said no. But I just want to try a little sip!

MOM: No. Coffee is not for children. I'm going to pay the check. I'll be back in a minute.

(MOM exits.)

CHARLIE: Dad, pleeeease? I just want to try it.

DAD: You won't like it.

CHARLIE: How do you know?

DAD: I'm pretty sure.

CHARLIE: Well, if I won't like it, why can't I just have a tiny sip?

DAISY: Charlie, you're so annoying!

CHARLIE: Please, Dad?

DAD: Well . . . OK. But don't tell your mom. You're not going to like it!

DAISY: Hey, if he can try it, I want to try it, too!

DAD: OK, fine. But hurry up. Your mother's going to be back at the table soon.

(CHARLIE and DAISY take quick sips out of DAD's cup.)

CHARLIE: Yuck! That's horrible!

DAD: I told you!

CHARLIE: It's so . . . yucky!

DAISY: It's bitter.

CHARLIE: Yeah, that's the word! Why do you drink that?

DAD: I don't know. I started drinking coffee in college, and I got used to the taste.

CHARLIE: Tastes like poison! I'll never drink it again!

DAD: Good! What did you think Daisy?

(DAISY smiles.)

DAISY: I liked it. A lot.

DAD: Uh-oh.

(MOM enters.)

MOM: OK, we're all set! Ready to go?

DAISY: Mom, can I finish your coffee?

MOM: We already discussed this. No coffee for kids!

DAISY: But I like it!

MOM: How do you know?

DAISY: I had some.

MOM: When?

DAISY: Dad let me try a teeny-weenie bit.

MOM: He did?!

DAD: Double uh-oh.

Questions

1. Should children drink coffee?

2. How do you feel when you are told that things are "just for grown-ups"?

3. Do you think Dad will get in trouble?

4. Who acts smarter in this play—Mom or Dad?

5. Is there anything you aren't allowed to do, eat, or drink?

6. Why do parents make rules?

7. Do you like it best when your mom and dad agree about the rules? Why or why not?

MINE, NOT YOURS

Everybody wants the cheesiest piece of pizza.
Who will get it?

Characters
Dad
Ty
Duncan
Olivia
Waitress

(TY, DUNCAN, OLIVIA, and DAD are sitting at a table in a restaurant.)

DAD: I'm hungry. How about you?

TY: I'm starving.

DUNCAN: I'm double starving.

OLIVIA: I'm the hungriest one here!

DAD: Here comes the pizza!

(WAITRESS enters with a pizza.)

WAITRESS: Here we are!

DAD: Thank you!

WAITRESS: Be careful. It's hot!

(WAITRESS leaves.)

DUNCAN: Let's dig in!

DAD: Hold on. The waitress said it was very hot, so let me serve you. Everybody hold out your plates. Ty, which piece do you want?

(TY holds out his plate and points to one piece near Duncan.)

TY: This piece here has the most cheese!

DUNCAN: I want it!

OLIVIA: Me, too!

DUNCAN: It's closest to me! Dad, it's mine!

DAD: There's enough for everybody. Take it easy, guys.

(WAITRESS comes back in. TY puts down his plate.)

WAITRESS: How is everything?

DAD: Fine, thank you.

WAITRESS: Can I get you more napkins?

DAD: Sure.

(WAITRESS exits.)

DUNCAN: I want that piece, Dad. Don't give it to Ty.

OLIVIA: Daddy, the boys get whatever they want. I never get the piece with the most cheese.

TY: I called it!

(The WAITRESS comes back in with more napkins.)

WAITRESS: Here you go! Anything else I can get you?

DUNCAN: How come there's always one piece that has more cheese?

WAITRESS: I don't know. I guess it just works out that way.

TY: Don't you think I should get the piece with the most cheese?

OLIVIA: That's not fair! He can't ask her!

DAD: OK, OK, everybody. Calm down. I'm going to give Ty this piece because he picked it first—

OLIVIA: That's because you asked him first!

DUNCAN: If you asked me first, I would have picked that piece, too!

DAD: That's enough.

WAITRESS: I think I should go.

DAD: Thank you.

(The WAITRESS exits.)

OLIVIA: So who gets the cheesy piece?

(DUNCAN licks his hand and touches the pizza.)

DUNCAN: Ouch! I do!

DAD: Duncan, what are you doing? The pizza is hot!

OLIVIA: Dad, he licked the pizza!

DUNCAN: I licked my hand, then I touched the pizza.

TY: That's cheating.

DUNCAN: But now that piece is mine.

TY: No, it's not.

DUNCAN: I licked it!

DAD: That wasn't very polite.

OLIVIA: That's gross! And unfair!

DAD: *(Sighs.)* OK, Duncan. Give me your plate. That piece you touched is yours.

TY: That's not fair!

DAD: But you are not to pull a stunt like that again, do you hear me?

DUNCAN: Yes, Dad. Ha, ha, you guys, I got the cheesy piece!

Questions

1. Who should have gotten the cheesy piece? Why?

2. Was Duncan's move (licking his hand then touching the pizza) smart? Gross? Rude? Impolite? Daring?

3. Should Duncan be punished?

4. If you were Dad, how would you get the kids to stop arguing? What would you think of Dad if he ate the piece of pizza everyone wanted?

5. Do you ever fight over food in your family?

6. What is it like to be the only girl or the only boy in a family?

7. In a large family, what is the best way to get what you want? Is it hard to be heard when you have a few brothers and sisters?

8. Would it be worse or the same if Duncan spit on the pizza? Would it be better or worse or the same if he stuck his finger in the pizza?

NO MANNERS

Miss Julia is not happy with Alex and Samantha's manners in the classroom.

Characters

Miss Julia
Alex
Samantha

(MISS JULIA is sitting behind a big desk. ALEX and SAMANTHA sit at a table next to her desk.)

MISS JULIA: Now you two know why you are here. Your behavior in class is not acceptable. Do you understand?

ALEX/SAMANTHA: Yes, Miss Julia.

MISS JULIA: I want the two of you to write a list of the things you have done wrong today.

(ALEX starts to pick his nose.)

MISS JULIA: Do you understand me—

(MISS JULIA sees what ALEX is doing.)

MISS JULIA: Excuse me! Alex! What are you doing?

ALEX: *(Still picking his nose.)* I am listening to you, Miss Julia.

MISS JULIA: Yes, and what else are you doing?

ALEX: *(Still picking his nose.)* I am sitting in a chair.

MISS JULIA: And what else?

SAMANTHA: You're picking your nose, Alex.

ALEX: Oh.

(ALEX stops picking his nose.)

MISS JULIA: That is better. Now where was I?

(SAMANTHA starts coughing.)

MISS JULIA: Are you OK, Samantha?

(SAMANTHA coughs some more, then turns around and makes a spitting sound.)

SAMANTHA: Yes. I feel better now.

MISS JULIA: Samantha! Did you just—Did you just spit on the floor?

SAMANTHA: I had something stuck in my throat.

MISS JULIA: That is—disgusting! Why did you do that?

SAMANTHA: Something was stuck in my throat.

MISS JULIA: Do you think it is OK to spit, Samantha?

SAMANTHA: My uncle Joe spits after he coughs. He also spits after he runs.

MISS JULIA: Your uncle Joe should not spit! No one should spit!

(*ALEX starts sniffing.*)

MISS JULIA: You two really need to learn some manners. Let's start on those lists.

(*ALEX sneezes and wipes his nose with his hands.*)

SAMANTHA: Ew!

MISS JULIA: Alex, do you need a tissue?

ALEX: No.

(*ALEX wipes his hands on his pants.*)

SAMANTHA: Ew.

ALEX: Shut up, Samantha.

(*ALEX pushes SAMANTHA. [IMPORTANT NOTE: In plays, no one ever really gets pushed or hurt. It's all pretend!] SAMANTHA stands and screams.*)

SAMANTHA: Miss Julia, Alex touched me! His hands had snot on them!

(*SAMANTHA starts coughing again.*)

MISS JULIA: Alex! You are not supposed to wipe your nose on your hands or push people!

SAMANTHA: Or push people with your snotty hands!

(SAMANTHA coughs on ALEX's face. ALEX stands and runs to the other side of the room.)

ALEX: Did you see that, Miss Julia? Samantha coughed on my face!

(MISS JULIA stands.)

MISS JULIA: You are both acting very poorly! Were you raised by wolves?

ALEX/SAMANTHA: How did you know?

MISS JULIA: You were raised by wolves?

SAMANTHA: Yes. I live with my grandma and grandpa. Their names are Mister and Misses Woolf.

ALEX: I live in a cave in the forest with animals.

MISS JULIA: Oh my. I think I need to sit down!

Questions

1. Do you think Alex is telling the truth?

2. What impolite things does Alex do?

3. What impolite things does Samantha do?

4. What should Miss Julia do to correct their behavior?

5. Why shouldn't you pick your nose? Why shouldn't you spit? Why shouldn't you wipe your nose on your hands or clothes? Why shouldn't you push people? Why shouldn't you cough without covering your mouth?

6. What does it feel like to sit next to someone doing one of things Alex and Samantha do?

7. Why do people pick their noses? Why do people spit? What are other things you can do instead?

8. Should Alex and Samantha be allowed to do whatever they want? Are people too sensitive about germs and politeness?

Part 2
SCARY!

What are these characters saying?
What's going on in this picture?
You decide!

SUDDENLY SICK

It is time to take a test and suddenly Suzy and Henry feel sick!

Characters

Mrs. Blitzen
Suzy
Henry
Marta

MRS. BLITZEN: Class, close your books. It's time for the test.

SUZY: The test?

HENRY: Oh no.

SUZY: Mrs. Blitzen?

MRS. BLITZEN: Yes, Suzy?

SUZY: I feel sick.

MRS. BLITZEN: After the test you can go to the nurse.

SUZY: But I need to go to the nurse now, Miss Blitzen!

MRS. BLITZEN: Just put your head down on the desk for a minute while I hand out the tests. See if you feel better.

SUZY: I won't! I know I won't!

MRS. BLITZEN: Very well. Go to the nurse, Suzy.

MARTA: I'll take her, Mrs. Blitzen.

MRS. BLITZEN: Can you get to the nurse by yourself, Suzy?

SUZY: I think I can.

MRS. BLITZEN: OK, then. Go ahead.

(SUZY exits. HENRY watches SUZY leave.)

HENRY: Mrs. Blitzen?

MRS. BLITZEN: Yes, Henry?

HENRY: I feel sick, too. I think I have the same thing as Suzy.

MARTA: No, he doesn't. He feels fine. He was playing tag during recess.

MRS. BLITZEN: That's enough, Marta. Now, Henry, do you think you might just be nervous about the test?

HENRY: No. I am really and truly sick, Mrs. Blitzen.

MRS. BLITZEN: I think you might be faking to get out of the test.

HENRY: No. I feel like I'm going to die. Or faint. Or throw up. Or all of those things. Maybe at the same time.

MARTA: You're going to die and throw up at the same time?

HENRY: It could happen.

MARTA: He's lying, Mrs. Blitzen.

MRS. BLITZEN: That's enough, Marta.

MARTA: I was just trying to help.

MRS. BLITZEN: I know you were, but that's enough. Now Henry, I think you're fine. Why don't you take a few deep breaths as I pass out the test.

HENRY: I feel dizzy.

MRS. BLITZEN: That's enough, Henry. You're fine.

HENRY: How come Suzy got to go to the nurse?

MRS. BLITZEN: Suzy was sick.

HENRY: She was faking! She wasn't sick at all. It's not fair. You believe her, and you don't believe me. You're going to feel very, very bad if I die, Mrs. Blitzen.

MRS. BLITZEN: Henry, quiet down and take the test. You're not going to die.

HENRY: Girls get away with everything. I hate being a boy!

Questions

1. Was Suzy pretending to be sick?

2. Why does the teacher believe Suzy, but not Henry?

3. Do girls get away with more than boys? Why or why not?

4. What do you think of Marta?

5. Why does the teacher say "that's enough" to Marta? Is Mrs. Blitzer not happy with Marta? Why?

6. Should Henry be allowed to go to the nurse?

HOMEWORK?

Alexandra forgets her homework.

Characters

Mr. Teller
Alexandra
Mya
Andrew

(ALEXANDRA, MYA, ANDREW, and MR. TELLER are in a classroom.)

MR. TELLER: Pass up your homework.

ALEXANDRA: Mya!

MYA: What is it?

ALEXANDRA: I forgot my homework!

MR. TELLER: No talking! Is something wrong, Alexandra?

ALEXANDRA: I lost my homework!

MR. TELLER: You lost it? Maybe it's in your desk. I think we should all clean our desks later this week. They are a mess.

ALEXANDRA: I just can't find it.

MR. TELLER: Keep looking.

ANDREW: Maybe her dog ate her homework. That happens to me a lot.

MR. TELLER: I know. Your dog must really love eating paper.

ANDREW: He does!

MYA: Maybe she dropped it on the way to school!

ALEXANDRA: Yeah! I think that might have happened! I was walking to school, and it was windy, and I saw something fly away—I bet it was my homework!

MR. TELLER: What was our homework, Alexandra?

ALEXANDRA: I was to . . . write . . . an . . .

MYA: *(Whispering.)* Essay!

MR. TELLER: Quiet, Miss Garcia.

MYA: Sorry.

ALEXANDRA: Our homework was to write an essay!

MR. TELLER: About what?

ALEXANDRA: About . . . how . . .

(MYA shakes her head no.)

ALEXANDRA: . . . when . . .

(MYA shakes her head no.)

ALEXANDRA: . . . where . . .

(MYA nods her head.)

ALEXANDRA: Where!

MR. TELLER: Where what, Miss Jones?

ALEXANDRA: Where . . .

(ALEXANDRA looks at MYA.)

MR. TELLER: Don't look at Miss Garcia.

(ALEXANDRA looks at ANDREW.)

ANDREW: Don't look at me! My dog ate my homework so I don't remember what it's about!

ALEXANDRA: I forget, too. But I did it!

MR. TELLER: Andrew and Alexandra, you stay after class.

ALEXANDRA: Why?

MR. TELLER: Because you did not do your homework.

ALEXANDRA: I did, too!

ANDREW: My dog ate it!

MR. TELLER: Both very good stories. But you are not telling the truth.

ANDREW: Never get a dog, Mr. Teller. It will ruin your life. I have not gone outside for recess in my whole life.

MR. TELLER: If you want to start going out for recess, you'll start doing your homework!

ALEXANDRA: I will never forget again!

MYA: See you later, Alexandra.

(MYA exits. ALEXANDRA puts her head down on her desk and starts to cry.)

ANDREW: Don't be sad, Alexandra. I do this every day. You just sit here and write.

ALEXANDRA: I want to go outside.

ANDREW: Me, too. What is recess like?

Questions

1. Have you ever gotten in trouble at school? How did it make you feel?

2. What do you think Alexandra should have done or said when Mr. Teller asked for the homework?

3. Do you think Andrew's dog really eats his homework?

4. Do you think Alexandra will ever forget her homework again?

5. Why does Alexandra lie about losing her homework?

6. Should Mya have tried to help her?

NO MORE!

Jordan meets up with a bully.

Characters
Jordan
Justin
Ellie
Vinnie

JORDAN: Let's go this way today.

JUSTIN: We can't go that way.

JORDAN: Why not?

JUSTIN: That's the way Vinnie goes.

JORDAN: So?

JUSTIN: So Vinnie will steal our lunches.

JORDAN: No, he won't! I'd hit him with my lunchbox before I'd let him take my lunch.

JUSTIN: You are new in school. So let me help you out. Do not ever go down this street. And do not ever mess with Vinnie. He's the meanest kid in all the world!

JORDAN: In all the world?

JUSTIN: Trust me.

(JORDAN turns and starts walking to the right.)

JUSTIN: Where are you going? Didn't you hear me? Stop!

(JORDAN stops and turns to look at JUSTIN.)

JORDAN: I heard you. I just think it's silly. This is the shorter way to school, right?

JUSTIN: Right. But—

(ELLIE enters.)

JORDAN: I'm going this way.

ELLIE: NO! What are you doing? Are you crazy? Justin, didn't you tell Jordan about Vinnie?

JUSTIN: I did! She won't listen!

JORDAN: You, too? Why is everyone so scared of Vinnie?

JUSTIN: Like I told you, he is the meanest—

ELLIE: —nastiest—

JUSTIN: —most terrible kid in all the world!

ELLIE: In the universe!

JORDAN: I think I have to meet this Vinnie. He wouldn't hit a girl, would he?

ELLIE: Yes, he would.

JORDAN: Let's see.

(JORDAN takes a few more steps to her right. ELLIE and JUSTIN slowly, carefully, quietly walk behind JORDAN.)

JORDAN: See? He's not even here. I don't know what you were all so—

(VINNIE pops up out of nowhere.)

VINNIE: Give me your lunches!

(ELLIE screams and runs away, exiting to the left. VINNIE laughs. JUSTIN holds out his lunch and closes his eyes. JORDAN does nothing.)

VINNIE: Thanks, dork.

(VINNIE takes JUSTIN's lunch.)

VINNIE: *(To JORDAN.)* Are you deaf? Give me your lunch!

JORDAN: I want my lunch.

VINNIE: So do I.

JORDAN: It's my lunch.

VINNIE: Not for long.

JORDAN: What are you going to do? Hit me?

VINNIE: Maybe.

JORDAN: Maybe I'll hit you first.

VINNIE: Ha ha h—

(JORDAN "hits" VINNIE in the face with her lunchbox. [IMPORTANT NOTE: In plays, no one ever really gets hit or hurt. It's all pretend!] VINNIE grabs his nose.)

VINNIE: Ow! Ow! Owie! You hurted me, you mean girl!

JORDAN: Go away!

(VINNIE runs away crying.)

JUSTIN: I can't believe you did that. You hit Vinnie Muller.

JORDAN: I have a cupcake in my lunch today. There is not a person in the world who can have my lunch today!

Questions

1. Did Jordan do the right thing when she hit Vinnie?

2. How should you deal with bullies?

3. Why are bullies mean to other kids?

4. Was Ellie smart to run away?

5. If you were Justin, would you help Jordan if Vinnie started bullying to her?

6. How should grown-ups punish bullies?

7. Does it help to tell grown-ups when a bully is bothering you?

TOO SHY

Everyone has been trying out for the school play, including shy Tim.

Characters

Miss O'Dell
Tim
Miranda
Louis

(MISS O'DELL stands in front of the class with a book in her hand.)

MISS O'DELL: Everyone will be standing up and reading a line to audition for the school play. Let's start with . . . Tim.

TIM: No—No thanks.

MISS O'DELL: Everyone will be auditioning, Tim.

TIM: Do I have to?

MISS O'DELL: Yes, but someone else can go first. Then maybe you'll see how easy it is. Who would like to come up and read the line first?

(After a moment, MIRANDA raises her hand.)

MISS O'DELL: Come on up, Miranda!

MIRANDA: What am I supposed to do, Miss O'Dell?

MISS O'DELL: Why don't you read this line, Miranda. Say it like you are very sad.

(MISS O'DELL hands the book to MIRANDA.)

MIRANDA: OK. *(Reading from the book.)* "You can't leave, Jimmy. You are my best friend."

MISS O'DELL: That was pretty good, Miranda. Can you say it even sadder?

MIRANDA: OK. *(Reading from the book very dramatically.)* "YOU CAN'T LEAVE, JIMMY! YOU ARE MY BEST FRIEND!!!!"

MISS O'DELL: That was good. Can you read it one more time—this time a little less sad?

MIRANDA: OK. "You can't leave, Jimmy! You are my best friend!"

MISS O'DELL: That was very good, Miranda. See how easy it is? Everyone, let's clap for Miranda. Good job!

(LOUIS and TIM clap. MIRANDA gives the book back to MISS O'DELL and sits down.)

MISS O'DELL: Who will be next? Louis? How about you?

(LOUIS stands up.)

LOUIS: *(Acts very upset—like he's crying.)* Jimmy, Jimmy, baby, don't leave—

MISS O'DELL: OK, Louis, very funny. I am going to give you a different line to read.

LOUIS: OK.

MISS O'DELL: Here it is. This is the character of Martin. He is an alligator who doesn't like anything or anyone.

LOUIS: Excellent! *(Takes the book from MISS O'DELL.)* "I don't want to play with Jimmy. He can't do anything right!"

MISS O'DELL: Great! Can you say it more like an alligator?

LOUIS: *(In a deeper voice.)* "I don't want to play with Jimmy. He can't do anything right!"

MISS O'DELL: Well done. You may sit down. Everyone clap for Louis!

(TIM and MIRANDA clap. LOUIS hands back the book and sits down.)

MISS O'DELL: OK, Tim, see how easy it is? Why don't you come up here? Don't be shy, Tim. It will be fine. Was it scary to audition, Miranda?

MIRANDA: No. Not really.

MISS O'DELL: How about you, Louis? Was auditioning hard for you?

LOUIS: No way! I'm gooooood.

MISS O'DELL: See? Come on up, Tim.

(TIM really, really doesn't want to stand up in front of the class, but he does.)

MISS O'DELL: Tim, read this line.

TIM: *(Very quietly.)* "I just want to go to the city."

MISS O'DELL: This is the role of Jimmy. He lives in a swamp, but he wants to live in a big city. He is telling his mother that he wants to move far, far away from home. Can you read it again, Tim? A little louder this time?

(TIM sighs. He is nervous and doesn't like being in front of everyone.)

MIRANDA: Don't be scared, Tim. You can do it!

(TIM looks at the book for a long time then looks up at MISS O'DELL.)

LOUIS: Hurry up, Tim! It's easy!

(TIM looks very serious and stares at the book again.)

MISS O'DELL: Go on, Tim. You're doing a wonderful job.

(TIM takes a deep breath.)

TIM: *(A little bit louder.)* "I just want to go to the city."

MISS O'DELL: Terrific, Tim! Everybody give Tim a hand!

(MIRANDA and LOUIS clap for TIM. TIM sits down quickly behind LOUIS and MIRANDA.)

MISS O'DELL: See? It wasn't that painful, was it, Tim?

(TIM buries his face in his hands.)

MISS O'DELL: Who is next? I think we are going to have a wonderful school play this year!

Questions

1. Why is Tim quiet for so long?

2. How do you think Tim feels when he looks up at Miss O'Dell before he reads his line the second time?

3. What is it like to be shy? What does it feel like to be scared to speak in front of other people?

4. Why are some people shy?

5. Do you think speaking in front of everyone is as easy for Tim as it is for Louis and Miranda?

6. What could Miss O'Dell do to make Tim feel better?

7. Do the other people in this scene—Louis, Miranda, and Miss O'Dell—understand how Tim feels?

NO NURSES!

Harvey is sick, but he does not want to go to the nurse.

Characters

Harvey
Neil
Tori
Mrs. Daniels

(HARVEY and NEIL are sitting next to each other at a table. TORI sits further away.)

HARVEY: *(Grabbing his stomach. Groaning.)* Oh.

NEIL: What's wrong.

HARVEY: Nothing.

NEIL: You look like you are going to barf.

TORI: Ew! Harvey is going to barf?

HARVEY: No.

TORI: You should go to the nurse. Now!

HARVEY: I don't want to go to the nurse.

NEIL: Why not?

HARVEY: I don't know. I don't like the nurse.

TORI: Our nurse is nice!

NEIL: Yeah. And you won't have to go to class!

HARVEY: But everyone treats you funny when you go to the nurse.

NEIL: What do you mean?

HARVEY: Everyone talks to you like, "Are you OK, Harvey?"

TORI: Well, you're sick. Of course everyone would say that!

HARVEY: Yeah, but then they look at you all sad like you're dying or something, too.

NEIL: So what?

HARVEY: I don't like people to feel sorry for me.

TORI: Maybe your mom or dad will pick you up, and you can go home!

HARVEY: That's the worst thing of all! Then everyone thinks you have cooties!

TORI: You do have cooties. All boys do.

NEIL: No, they don't!

TORI: You do, too!

(HARVEY grabs his stomach.)

HARVEY: Ooooooh.

TORI: Uh-oh. He's totally going to barf.

HARVEY: No, I'm not!

NEIL: Go to the bathroom now. Before you barf all over everyone in the lunchroom. Then everyone will definitely look at you funny.

HARVEY: No, I think I'm OK.

TORI: Harvey! Go! Fast!

HARVEY: Promise you won't tell anyone?

NEIL: Go!

HARVEY: Promise you won't tell!

NEIL: Why?

HARVEY: I don't want to go to the nurse!

NEIL: OK, fine! Just go!

(HARVEY starts to run away. MRS. DANIELS stops him.)

MRS. DANIELS: Harvey, we do not run in the cafeteria!

HARVEY: I gotta go!

TORI: Mrs. Daniels, you have to let him go!

MRS. DANIELS: Why?

NEIL: Trust us. It's important!

MRS. DANIELS: Harvey is not going anywhere until I get an explanation!

TORI: He's gonna barf!

(MRS. DANIELS lets go of HARVEY's arm right away. HARVEY runs away.)

NEIL: Ooooooo, Tori, Harvey is going to be so mad at you.

TORI: Why?

MRS. DANIELS: Neil, why don't you go make sure Harvey's OK. Make sure he goes to the nurse's office.

NEIL: That's why, Tori!

(NEIL exits.)

TORI: I hope Harvey made it to the bathroom.

Questions

1. Why doesn't Harvey want to go to the nurse?

2. Can you understand how Harvey feels?

3. Do you think Harvey will be mad at Tori for telling?

4. What do you think is wrong with Harvey?

5. Do you like going to the nurse?

6. Do you like it when people feel sorry for you?

LOST

Finn, Connor, and Josh get lost on the way home from school.

Characters

Finn
Connor
Josh
Officer McMann
Pregnant lady
Josh's mom

(FINN, CONNOR, and JOSH enter.)

FINN: My brother told me that second grade was hard, but it's not so bad.

CONNOR: Yeah. It's easy! Right, Josh?

JOSH: Yeah. Sure.

FINN: The new stuff we are learning is actually pretty cool.

CONNOR: I got a check plus and a gold star on my spelling test.

FINN: You're quiet in class this year, Josh.

JOSH: Yeah, well . . .

FINN: Hey, where are we?

CONNOR: I don't know. Have we ever been here before?

JOSH: I don't think so.

FINN: We must have made a wrong turn.

CONNOR: What should we do?

FINN: Let's ask directions.

JOSH: Which person should we ask?

CONNOR: How about that police officer? *(Points to the left.)*

FINN: What about that pregnant lady? (*Points to the right.)*

JOSH: My mom always said, "Don't talk to strangers."

FINN: But we're lost!

CONNOR: My mom told me to ask a police officer.

JOSH: What if he's not a real police officer?

FINN: That's why I said to ask the pregnant lady. Pregnant ladies don't kidnap kids.

JOSH: Maybe they do.

FINN: She's pregnant! She has her own baby.

JOSH: Maybe she wants more.

CONNOR: I think we should ask the police officer.

JOSH: There are three of us. I guess we'll be safe.

(OFFICER McMANN enters. JOSH, CONNOR, and FINN walk over to him.)

CONNOR: Excuse me, Officer?

OFFICER McMANN: Yes? Can I help you boys?

JOSH: Are you a real police officer?

OFFICER McMANN: Yes, I am! Just passed my police officer test last week.

FINN: Can you tell us where Mulberry Street is? We got lost.

OFFICER McMANN: This is my first day on the job. I don't know where Mulberry Street is. I'm sorry! Are you boys lost?

CONNOR: Yes.

OFFICER McMANN: Let's ask that pregnant lady.

FINN: I told them that's what we should do in the first place!

(PREGNANT LADY enters.)

OFFICER McMANN: Excuse me, ma'am, do you know where Mulberry Street is? These boys are lost.

PREGNANT LADY: Yes, I do! Mulberry Street is two blocks back that way. *(Points to the right.)* You passed it!

FINN/CONNOR/JOSH: Thank you!

OFFICER McMANN: Can you boys find your way home from there?

CONNOR: Yes, sir!

(JOSH'S MOM enters, holding a grocery bag. OFFICER McMANN and PREGNANT LADY exit.)

JOSH'S MOM: Josh! What are you doing here?

JOSH: We got lost! I'm sorry, Mom, you told me never to talk to strangers, but we asked a police officer for help.

JOSH'S MOM: Well, I'm glad you boys are OK. Do you want a ride home?

FINN: That would be great!

JOSH'S MOM: My car is right over there.

(FINN and CONNOR exit.)

JOSH: Mom?

JOSH'S MOM: Yes?

JOSH: I have to tell you something.

JOSH'S MOM: What is it?

JOSH: Everyone gets what we're learning in school, and I think it's hard. I think I might be . . . dumb.

JOSH'S MOM: Josh, you're not dumb! Did you tell the teacher that you didn't understand?

JOSH: Mom . . . everyone else gets it. If I tell the teacher I don't understand, everyone will think I'm stupid.

JOSH'S MOM: I bet a lot of other students feel like you do. You can't be afraid to ask questions! That's the teacher's job—to teach you and to answer your questions. But let's see if I can help you tonight. Sound good?

JOSH: Sounds great!

JOSH'S MOM: Get in the car. Let's go home, Josh.

JOSH: Thanks, Mom.

Questions

1. Josh is lost in two ways in this scene. Can you name both ways he gets lost?

2. If you were lost, who is the best person to ask for help? Should Finn, Connor, and Josh have asked the police officer or the pregnant lady for help?

3. Were the boys safe, since they were together?

4. What should you do if a stranger asks you a question?

5. Was it safe for Connor and Finn to go home with Josh's mom?

6. What should Connor do about being confused in school? Was his mother's advice good?

7. Are you ever afraid to ask questions in class? Why?

8. Do you think other kids in school feel the same as Josh does?

WHOOPS!

Tony and Karen are playing catch in the house. Guess what happens next!

Characters

Teresa
Karen
Tony

(TONY and KAREN are throwing a ball in a living room. TERESA is watching.)

TERESA: You guys are not supposed to play catch in the house.

KAREN: Says who?

TERESA: Says me.

TONY: You are not the boss of us!

TERESA: Says Mom and Dad, too.

(TONY and KAREN stop playing.)

KAREN: We're not hurting anybody.

TERESA: You might.

TONY: We won't!

TERESA: Well, don't tell me if you break your legs or anything. I won't take you to the hospital!

KAREN: No one is going to get their legs broken, Teresa!

TONY: *(Talking to TERESA.)* Maybe you!

TERESA: Are you threatening me? Because I will tell Mom.

KAREN: Don't be so serious. We're just having fun!

TERESA: Well, I'm going to be in trouble if anything happens.

TONY: Why?

TERESA: Because I'm the—

KAREN: You're the oldest. You're the oldest. We know! You tell us that all the time. It's boring.

TERESA: Well, it's true. I am the oldest so I'm responsible when Mom and Dad are gone.

TONY: You wish!

(TONY throws the ball to KAREN, and they start playing catch again.)

TERESA: Nobody listens to me!

(TERESA starts to leave the room. Suddenly, there is a crashing sound—the ball broke a vase.)

TERESA: See! I told you!

TONY: It was an accident!

TERESA: Now you're going to be in trouble.

TONY: I didn't throw the ball that time!

KAREN: I didn't mean to hit the vase!

TERESA: Mom and Dad are going to be so mad at you two.

KAREN: I thought they were going to be mad at you.

TERESA: I'll tell them that you were playing catch, and I told you to stop, and you wouldn't listen.

KAREN: I'll tell them that you were playing catch, and I told you to stop, and you wouldn't listen.

TERESA: They won't believe that!

TONY: Maybe they will. Maybe we'll say that you were playing with the ball all by yourself.

TERESA: That doesn't even make sense. You guys are so mean! *(Starts to get upset.)* I was telling the truth. You guys are lying! This isn't fair. I wasn't playing with the ball at all!

KAREN: Calm down.

TONY: Yeah, take it easy!

KAREN: Just help us figure out what to do.

TERESA: I don't know what to do.

TONY: Can we fix it?

KAREN: Yeah!

TERESA: No.

TONY: Why not?

TERESA: There are too many pieces.

KAREN: We could try.

TERESA: Plus, we're not allowed to touch the really good glue.

TONY: Why not?

TERESA: If you get it on your hands, your skin will stick to whatever you touch. So if you get the glue on your hands and you touch your face, your hand will get stuck on your face!

KAREN: And if you stick your hand to a knife, you'll have a knife hand!

TONY: Cool! And if you stick your hand to your butt—

TERESA: Don't be silly, Tony.

TONY: Why not?

KAREN: We have to fix the vase!

TERESA: I don't think we can fix it.

TONY: Then what do we do?

KAREN: Shhhh! Mom and Dad are home. What do we do?

TONY: Hide!

(TERESA, KAREN, and TONY run off in different directions, leaving the room.)

Questions

1. What do you think happens next?

2. Do Karen and Tony get in trouble?

3. Does Teresa get in trouble?

4. What do you think of Teresa? What is she like as a person?

5. What do you think about Tony and Karen. Do you like them?

6. What do you think Tony, Karen, and Teresa should do about the broken vase?

7. Do you think oldest or only children get more responsibility? Is that good or bad? Can older or only children do things younger siblings can't do?

8. Do you think younger children get away with more? Can they do more or less than older siblings or only children?

9. If something is an accident, should you be punished for doing it?

THE DEEP END

Penny does not want to go into the deep end of the swimming pool.

Characters

Fred
Penny
Dad

(PENNY is in her bathing suit. FRED, the lifeguard, enters.)

FRED: OK, Penny. For your swimming lesson today, you are going to get into the deep end of the pool.

PENNY: The deep end?

FRED: Yes. You've been practicing for a long time. You are ready.

PENNY: I don't think I'm ready.

FRED: You remember how to tread water?

PENNY: A little.

FRED: How to float on your back?

PENNY: I guess so.

FRED: How to do the doggy paddle?

PENNY: I'm not that good at it.

FRED: You're ready. Come on. Let's go!

PENNY: Could we just do another day by the steps?

FRED: Penny, I promise I'll be right there to help you if you get in trouble. But you are a good swimmer now! You shouldn't worry.

PENNY: I think I need more practice.

FRED: I'm the teacher, Penny. I think you are ready!

(PENNY thinks for a minute, unsure about what to do.)

PENNY: I don't know.

FRED: Look, your dad is right over there. He believes you can do it. I believe you can do it!

PENNY: I don't know. I'm just—I don't think I want to.

FRED: Why not?

PENNY: I just . . . I don't think I want to.

FRED: Are you scared?

PENNY: No! I mean . . . maybe.

FRED: I told you that I would be right there with you. Would I let you drown?

PENNY: I don't know.

FRED: You think I'd let you drown, right in front of me?

(PENNY starts to smile.)

PENNY: No. I guess not.

FRED: Just try it. Try it once. We'll stay in the deep end for five minutes, then come back to the shallow end by the steps.

PENNY: I like it by the steps. Then if I swallow water, I can get out fast.

FRED: I know. But sometimes you have to take risks.

PENNY: Why?

FRED: If you only did what felt easy to you all the time, well, you'd just sit around watching TV all day!

PENNY: That sounds good!

FRED: No, it doesn't, Penny. That might be fun for a little while, but you would get bored.

PENNY: I don't think I would. I like TV.

FRED: Think about all you would be missing! You wouldn't meet any new people. You wouldn't see snow or flowers or grass—

PENNY: I could look out the window.

FRED: Penny, I promise you it's good to scare
yourself a little bit sometimes. Especially when it
is safe. And I promise you that you will be safe.
Come on, let's just try. Will you try for me,
Penny?

PENNY: Well . . .

(DAD enters.)

DAD: I'm so proud of you, Penny. Fred says that
you are going to go into the deep end of the pool
today! I never learned to swim, and I always
regretted it. Once, I got invited to spend a summer with my friend Jack, but I told my mother I
didn't want to go. I was scared to go because I
couldn't swim. I always was sad that I didn't get
to go to the beach with Jack that summer. That
is why I want you to learn how to swim.

(PENNY takes a long, deep breath.)

PENNY: OK, Fred. I'm ready. I think.

FRED: Let's go into the deep end!

DAD: You're a brave girl, Penny!

Questions

1. Is there anything that scares you?

2. Do you think Fred is right? Is it good to try new things and do things that scare you sometimes?

3. Do you think you would like sitting home watching TV all the time? Why or why not?

4. Should Penny go into the deep end or should Penny stay safe by the steps on the shallow end? Why?

5. What things have you done that scared you?

6. When should you not do something that scares you?

7. Do you know anyone who seems fearless? Is that a good or bad way to be? Can being fearless ever be dangerous? Can being fearless ever be wonderful?

Part 3
SNEAKY!

What are these characters saying?
What's going on in this picture?
You decide!

THE PEN

Dylan, Sam, and Myles see something they want, but they don't have the money to buy it!

Characters

Sam
Dylan
Myles

(SAM is holding a pen.)

SAM: Hey, look at this!

DYLAN: Whoa. That is a nice pen.

MYLES: A pen is a pen. Big deal.

SAM: No, this pen can write on the moon. It can write upside down.

MYLES: So?

DYLAN: Normal pens can't do that!

SAM: This is what astronauts use. In space!

MYLES: Oh.

DYLAN: Does anyone have money? We could buy it and test it out!

MYLES: I don't have money.

SAM: Me neither. But . . . maybe we don't need money!

DYLAN: What do you mean?

SAM: It's just a pen, right?

DYLAN: Right.

SAM: And it probably doesn't cost that much, to a grown-up.

MYLES: Right, but we're kids.

SAM: Exactly. So maybe we should just take it. There's lot of pens here. They won't miss this one. And it doesn't cost that much.

DYLAN: Sam, we'll get in trouble.

MYLES: We could get arrested.

SAM: No, we couldn't!

DYLAN: Yes, we could!

SAM: It's just a pen! I'll just put it in my pocket.

(SAM puts the pen in his pocket.)

DYLAN: We're going to get in so much trouble. I'm going to pretend like I don't know you.

MYLES: No one's looking. Maybe it will be OK.

DYLAN: The alarm in the store will go off.

SAM: We can test it at my house.

MYLES: Who gets to keep it?

SAM: Me! It's in my pocket! Let's go.

(MYLES and SAM start walking.)

DYLAN: I'm not going with you!

(MYLES and SAM keep walking.)

DYLAN: Wait up!

(DYLAN catches up.)

DYLAN: The alarm is going to go off, and we'll be arrested and go to jail.

(MYLES, SAM, and DYLAN stop.)

SAM: We're out! See, nothing happened. No one's going to jail.

DYLAN: But what if our parents find out?

SAM: How will they find out?

DYLAN: I don't know.

MYLES: They won't find out if you don't tell them. Let's go test it out!

DYLAN: Let's get out of here before anyone notices the pen is gone!

SAM: No one's going to notice, silly!

MYLES: I'm going to try using it in a tree.

SAM: I want to try the pen upside down.

DYLAN: Come on, let's go, you guys!

Questions

1. What is the topic of this story?

2. Is it worse to take something that costs a lot of money?

3. What do you think will happen to Sam, Dylan, and Myles? Will they get into trouble or will nothing happen?

4. Can you think of a situation where it might be OK to take something that's not yours?

5. What do you think of Dylan? Would he be a good or bad friend to have?

6. What do you think of Sam? Would he be a good or bad friend to have?

TROUBLE MAKER

Molly cannot seem to be quiet in class.
Why doesn't she ever get in trouble?

Characters

Molly
Dani
Mr. Kidder
Cara
Roger
Michelle

MOLLY: What page are we on?

DANI: Page sixteen.

MR. KIDDER: Dani, no talking in class! Stay after class.

DANI: Thanks a lot, Molly!

MOLLY: Sorry!

(ROGER, CARA, MICHELLE, and DANI read quietly.)

MOLLY: Psst! Cara! Are we supposed to answer the questions at the end?

CARA: We're not supposed to talk in class!

MOLLY: I just want to know if we're supposed to answer the questions at the end.

CARA: Yes! Now don't ask me any more questions because I don't want to get in—

MR. KIDDER: Cara, are you talking in class? What did I just say to Dani?

CARA: You told her not to talk in class. But—

MR. KIDDER: No buts. There is no talking in class! Cara, you will stay after class.

MOLLY: He said no butts! That's a bad word!

(ROGER laughs.)

MR. KIDDER: Roger! You are supposed to be reading silently!

ROGER: You said, "No butts!"

MR. KIDDER: Roger, you will stay after class today. Does everyone want to stay after class with me?

DANI/CARA/ROGER/MICHELLE/MOLLY: No, Mr. Kidder.

MR. KIDDER: Then let's go back to our quiet reading.

(DANI, CARA, ROGER, MICHELLE, and MOLLY read quietly.)

MOLLY: He sure is mad.

(No one answers her.)

MOLLY: I thought his head was going to explode.

(No one answers her.)

MOLLY: I think Mr. Kidder looks like a panda.

(ROGER laughs.)

MR. KIDDER: Roger, you are already staying after class. Keep this up, and you'll be going to the principal's office.

ROGER: Sorry, Mr. Kidder.

(DANI, CARA, and ROGER read quietly.)

MICHELLE: I'm telling Mr. Kidder you said that, Molly.

MOLLY: I like pandas. I didn't say anything bad.

MICHELLE: Mr. Kidder?

MR. KIDDER: Is this important, Michelle? You should be reading quietly.

MICHELLE: I know, but Molly said you look like a panda.

MR. KIDDER: Michelle, stay after class and we will talk about tattling on other people.

MICHELLE: But she said you look like—

MR. KIDDER: Pandas are very majestic and rare.

MICHELLE: But—

MR. KIDDER: Read quietly, Michelle.

(A bell rings.)

MR. KIDDER: Class is over. Um . . . it seems everyone must stay after class with me except for . . . Molly. Molly, you may go.

ROGER: Hey!

DANI: That's not fair!

MR. KIDDER: Molly was the only one doing quiet reading today. You may leave, Molly.

(As MOLLY exits, DANI, CARA, ROGER, and MICHELLE all give her dirty looks.)

MOLLY: See you later, everybody!

Questions

1. Have you ever gotten in trouble for talking in class when you were trying to help someone else like Dani did?

2. Have you ever gotten in trouble for talking in class when you told someone else to be quiet like Cara?

3. Have you ever gotten in trouble in class for laughing at someone else's joke like Roger did?

4. Have you ever gotten in trouble for telling on someone else for doing something wrong like Michelle did?

5. Should Molly have gotten in trouble?

6. Why doesn't Molly get in trouble?

7. Was anyone punished unfairly?

8. What is Mr. Kidder like as a teacher?

THE TEST

Kyra didn't know there was a test today. What will she do? Maybe her friends can help.

Characters

Kyla
Emily
Vivian

KYLA: There's a test?

EMILY: Yes!

KYLA: Today?

EMILY: Yes. Didn't you know? I'm nervous.

KYLA: I didn't know! When did the teacher say there was a test?

VIVIAN: About a million times.

KYLA: What is it on?

VIVIAN: Everything.

EMILY: I studied, but I'm nervous.

KYLA: I don't remember the teacher saying anything about a test—What am I going to do?

EMILY: You're in trouble . . .

KYLA: What am I going to do, Emily?

VIVIAN: You'll probably fail.

KYLA: I can't fail! I'll get in trouble!

VIVIAN: What else can you do?

KYLA: You guys studied, right?

EMILY: Right.

VIVIAN: So?

KYLA: So you can help me pass the test!

EMILY: How?

VIVIAN: We're almost at school. There's no time to study.

KYLA : No, you could let me . . . I could see the answers on your papers.

EMILY: Cheat?!

KYLA : No, no! You would be helping me!

VIVIAN: That's cheating.

KYLA : No! I always get good grades. I'd get a good grade on this test, too, if I knew about it. You're just helping me. So I don't get into trouble.

EMILY: I think that's cheating.

VIVIAN: That's cheating, Kyla.

KYLA : You won't help me? I thought you were my friends!

EMILY: I am your friend!

KYLA : Then help me! Please, please, Emily?

EMILY: I don't know . . .

KYLA : Vivian, will you help me?

VIVIAN: That's cheating, Kyla. I don't think I can help you.

KYLA : Then you're not my friend anymore.

VIVIAN: Fine, cheater!

KYLA : You can't tell anyone, Vivian, or I'll tell then you wet your pants at Emily's sleepover!

VIVIAN: You wouldn't!

KYLA : I might.

VIVIAN: Goodbye forever, Kyla!

(VIVIAN walks away.)

EMILY: You wouldn't really tell, would you?

KYLA : No. So will you help me, Emily? Pleeeeease?

EMILY: Well . . . OK. I guess.

KYLA : Thank you, thank you, thank you! You're my best friend ever!

Questions

1. What would you do in Kyla's situation?

2. What would you do if you were Emily or Vivian? Would you help Kyla?

3. Have you ever forgotten about a test? What did you do?

4. Why do teachers give students tests?

5. Do you think Emily or Kyla will get in trouble?

6. Will Emily be cheating or helping a friend?

7. Is Vivian brave or mean for refusing to help?

8. What do you think about Kyla when she says to Vivian, "You can't tell anyone, Vivian, or I'll tell then you wet your pants at Emily's sleepover!"

9. Does it matter that Kyla usually gets good grades on her tests?

ROLY-POLY ROLAND

Dirk doesn't like vegetables, but his dog Roland does!

Characters

Mom
Dirk
Roland the Dog

MOM: Dirk! Come to dinner!
(DIRK enters.)

DIRK: What are we having tonight, Mom?

MOM: We're having Brussels sprouts, broccoli, and chicken.

DIRK: Is that it?

MOM: Oh, yes, and I made a salad, too. We're eating extra healthy now, remember?

DIRK: I wish I could forget. Do we have to eat healthy every day?

MOM: Yes, we do.

DIRK: Yuck. Can I get a hamburger?

MOM: Dirk, don't you want to grow up to be big and strong?

DIRK: No.

MOM: Don't give me attitude, young man.

DIRK: Mom, pleeeease can't I have a hot dog or
something, anything, else?

MOM: You're going to eat the dinner I made for you.

*(DIRK groans and sits at the table. ROLAND
enters. MOM exits to get the food.)*

DIRK: Hello, Roland! Good boy! Are you hungry,
Roland?

*(ROLAND barks. MOM enters with a big plate
of food.)*

MOM: Here you go, Dirk. I want you to clean your
plate.

DIRK: Mooooom. I hate this stuff.

MOM: No more complaining, Dirk! You'll eat what
you're given! It's all good, healthy stuff to help
you grow.

DIRK: I really don't care if I'm short.

MOM: You will. All the other boys will be tall and
growing, and you'll only be as tall as their belly
buttons.

DIRK: That's impossible.

MOM: No, it's not. Start eating!

DIRK: Can I make myself a peanut butter sandwich?

MOM: For the last time—

(The phone rings.)

MOM: I'll go answer that. Start eating. It tastes worse when it's cold.

(MOM exits.)

DIRK: *(Picking at his food.)* Yuck, yuck, yuck, yuck, yuck!

(ROLAND moans and begs.)

DIRK: Do you want some, Roland? Want some, boy? Hurry up, eat it before Mom gets back!

(DIRK puts his plate on the floor and ROLAND gobbles down everything.)

DIRK: Good boy! Thank you!

(ROLAND barks proudly and pants happily.)

DIRK: Shhh! Mom is coming back!

(MOM enters.)

MOM: Dirk, I told you to eat those vegetables or else you won't be able to play basketball with the other—Oh! You ate them all! Good boy!

DIRK: Thanks, Mom. I'm still hungry, though.

MOM: Well, I'll make you a hot dog. I'm so proud of you for eating your vegetables!

DIRK: Thanks, Mom.

MOM: Roland, do you want your dinner now?

(ROLAND barks.)

MOM: Hmmm. I think Roland might be getting a little bit fat. I'm feeding him the same food as always. Why is he getting bigger? Do you think Roland is getting chubby, Dirk?

DIRK: I think Roland is perfect. He looks extra healthy to me.

(ROLAND barks. MOM exits.)

DIRK: You're a good, good boy, Roland.

Questions

1. What do you think about Dirk?

2. Would feed your food to the dog, like Dirk does?

3. Is it good to feed people food to animals?

4. Is Dirk mean to his mother? How do you feel about the way Dirk tricks his mother?

5. Do you think Dirk will ever get caught feeding Roland? What do you think will happen if he does?

6. Should Dirk's mother give him a hot dog at the end?

7. Should Mom cook food Dirk likes better?

BEDTIME

Claudia and Brian want to stay up late;
Mom wants them to go to bed.

Characters

Mom
Brian
Claudia

(BRIAN, MOM and CLAUDIA sit together on a sofa.)

MOM: Time for bed!

BRIAN: Aw, Mom, do we have to? I just want to watch one more show.

MOM: Yes, you have to. Let's go. Upstairs! It's time.

BRIAN: Can we have just five more minutes?

MOM: Nope. It's bedtime!

BRIAN: Mooooooooom . . .

MOM: Briiiiiiiiiiaaaaaan . . .

BRIAN: I promise I won't be tired in the morning if you let me stay up later. I'll go right to sleep!

MOM: Get up. Let's march, young man. Get those legs moving.

BRIAN: Pleeeeeease?

MOM: No more whining. I'm serious. I want you in bed in one minute.

BRIAN: Does Claudia get to stay up?

MOM: No. Come on, Claudia. You, too.

CLAUDIA: I'm going.

MOM: Now. Get moving.

CLAUDIA: I'm moving. I'm just moving verrrrrry slowly.

MOM: Nice try. Now if you don't get upstairs now, there will be no TV tomorrow.

(BRIAN runs away very quickly.)

MOM: Claudia? I mean it. No TV tomorrow.

CLAUDIA: My foot is asleep.

MOM: You are full of excuses. You are starting to upset me now.

CLAUDIA: It really is asleep!

MOM: You're going to be sorry tomorrow if you don't go to bed now. One, I will be very upset with you. Two, you will be very tired tomorrow. Three, no TV tomorrow—

CLAUDIA: But Mom, I am moving!

MOM: Well, you better start moving a lot faster.

(BRIAN enters.)

BRIAN: Hey, if Claudia can stay up late, I want to stay up late, too!

MOM: No one is staying up late!

BRIAN: She's still sitting on the sofa.

MOM: Well, she is moving now. Or she better be.

BRIAN: Mom, I don't think I can sleep.

MOM: Why not?

BRIAN: Mike Maroni told me this story in school about a guy who went swimming in the ocean and a fish ate his foot!

MOM: Brian, you're not even near an ocean.

BRIAN: But I think there might be a big fish under my bed.

MOM: There's not a big fish under your bed.

BRIAN: Are you sure?

MOM: Yes! Now everyone get in bed NOW! I mean it. Let's go NOW.

BRIAN: OK. If I have to. Will you look under my bed?

MOM: Yes, Brian. But I know there isn't a big fish there. Fish live in water.

BRIAN: I know . . .

MOM: Claudia . . .

CLAUDIA: *(Standing.)* Mom, all the other kids in my class get to stay up later than me.

MOM: All the other kids in your class don't have me as their mother.

CLAUDIA: I know.

MOM: Get in your PJ's, and I'll come tuck you in. Up you go.

CLAUDIA: OK, Mom.

BRIAN: Mom? You're the best mom ever, even if we do have to go to bed too early.

MOM: Thank you, Brian.

Questions

1. Are there any reasons not to go to bed that Brian and Claudia haven't thought of?

2. Why do kids like to stay up past their bedtimes?

3. What is your bedtime?

4. What could Mom say or do to get Claudia and Brian to go to bed?

5. How do you think Mom feels when Brian and Claudia don't listen to her?

6. Does it matter when you go to bed? Why?

Part 4
NO FAIR!

What are these characters saying?
What's going on in this picture?
You decide!

THE CAT'S BEST FRIEND

Hannah's cat, Dilly, won't do what she wants.
And does Dilly like Hannah's brother best?

Characters

Hannah
Greg

HANNAH: Here, kitty, kitty, kitty. She won't come out from under the bed! She won't play with me! I hate this cat!

GREG: Hannah, she's just a kitten. She's scared.

HANNAH: I don't care. She's my kitten, and I want her to come sit on my lap!

GREG: Do you do everything Mom says?

HANNAH: Well, most of the time I do.

GREG: But not all of the time.

HANNAH: No, not all of the time.

GREG: See?

HANNAH: So what? That doesn't prove anything, Greg.

GREG: Does Mom ask you to come sit on her lap all the time?

HANNAH: No.

GREG: What if she did?

HANNAH: That doesn't make any sense. I'm a
human girl.

GREG: You'd hate it, right?

HANNAH: I guess so.

GREG: Well, that's what you want Dilly to do. You
want her to sit on your lap all the time. She must
be sick of it!

HANNAH: I'm nice to her! I'm the nicest person in
the whole house to her! It's not fair! She should
like me, too.

GREG: Maybe she just has a different way of
showing it. She doesn't bite you or scratch you,
does she?

HANNAH: No. But that's not good enough. She's
my cat, and I want Dilly to love me and sit on
my lap and let me pet her.

GREG: You're impossible. You're so bossy. You
always want things to go exactly your way. I
can't talk to you. That's why Dilly likes me best.

HANNAH: She does not!

GREG: She does, too. I'm the one she plays with the
most. We run around and play all the time.

HANNAH: So what? Does she let you pet her?

GREG: Well, duh. Of course. You've seen it!

HANNAH: That doesn't prove anything.

GREG: She follows me around all the time, too.

HANNAH: So?

GREG: So, she likes me best. Because I play with her, and I don't bother her all the time.

HANNAH: Greg, you're stupid. That's not true.

GREG: It is!

HANNAH: You're being mean.

GREG: I'm telling the truth.

HANNAH: I'm telling Mom.

GREG: What are you going to tell her? I didn't do anything to you!

HANNAH: You're being mean and hurting my feelings and telling big, fat lies!

(HANNAH pushes GREG. [IMPORTANT NOTE: In plays, no one ever gets pushed or hit or hurt for real. It's all pretend!])

GREG: I'm telling Mom you pushed me.

HANNAH: You made me do it. I couldn't help it! You made me.

GREG: No, I didn't. That doesn't make sense. You're stupid.

HANNAH: No, I'm not! I'm telling Mom you said I was stupid.

GREG: You said it to me first, stupid.

HANNAH: You are gonna be sooooo much trouble!

GREG: You pushed me. I think you'll be in trouble.

HANNAH/GREG: Mom!

Questions

1. Who do you think is the cat's best friend? Why?

2. Do you think it's right to make an animal do what you want to do? When might it be a good idea to boss a pet around?

3. Is Hannah right or wrong to push Greg? Why does she do it?

4. How does Hannah feel about the cat? How does Hannah feel about Greg?

5. Who do you think is older: Hannah or Greg?

6. Do you have a pet? Have you ever felt like Hannah or Greg?

7. Do you have a brother or sister? Have you ever felt like Hannah or Greg?

8. Who do you think the Mom will side with? Which person is right or are they both wrong?

9. Which is worse: Calling someone a name or pushing someone?

10. Do you think Dilly, the cat, can understand this argument? Can animals understand people?

RAJAH'S LAST DAY

Michael's goldfish Rajah isn't moving. Is this Rajah's last day on earth?

Character

Michael
Nina

MICHAEL: Rajah isn't moving. Do you think he's resting?

NINA: No.

MICHAEL: Maybe he's sleeping.

NINA: He's not.

MICHAEL: Maybe he just got tired of swimming. I don't know how fish can swim all day and night.

NINA: Fish rest. But Rajah's not resting.

MICHAEL: How do you know?

NINA: He's floating on the top. He's dead.

MICHAEL: No, he's not! He can't be!

NINA: He is.

MICHAEL: You think you know everything. I've only had Rajah for two weeks. He can't be dead. That would be the shortest life ever.

NINA: You don't know how old he was when you got him.

MICHAEL: He was young! He was swimming fast!

NINA: Maybe he was old.

MICHAEL: He wasn't old!

NINA: Well, fish don't live very long.

MICHAEL: Some do!

NINA: Not goldfish. Goldfish don't live long at all.

MICHAEL: He can't be dead!

NINA: Of course he can.

MICHAEL: But—I don't want him to be dead. I was going to get him a friend to swim with when I'm at school.

NINA: I'm sure Dad will get you a new fish.

MICHAEL: I don't want a new fish! I want Rajah. How do you know he's not sleeping?

NINA: They sleep at the bottom of the tank, not the top.

MICHAEL: How do you know?

NINA: We studied fish in school, and Mr. Jenkins has a fish tank.

MICHAEL: This isn't fair. I just got Rajah!

NINA: That's why we should get a turtle instead. They live longer. Come on; let's flush Rajah down the toilet.

MICHAEL: What?

NINA: That's what you do with fish.

MICHAEL: No way. Flush him down the toilet?

NINA: Yes!

MICHAEL: No way!

NINA: Why not?

MICHAEL: That's cruel! Think of all the things that get flushed down the toilet. Is that where you'd want to live forever?

NINA: But he's not alive. He's dead, Michael.

MICHAEL: Nina, that's wrong.

NINA: He's going to fish heaven. He's dead.

MICHAEL: But his body—It just doesn't seem right. We should bury him. In the backyard.

NINA: Ew!

MICHAEL: That's more disgusting than flushing him down the toilet? Rajah was a good fish. He deserves to be buried like a person.

NINA: So you wanna just put him in a hole and cover him up? That doesn't seem nicer than—

MICHAEL: No, we have to find a box for him.

NINA: He's not alive. He doesn't need a bedroom.

MICHAEL: Come on, Nina. Help me find a box!

NINA: OK, fine. But I still think we should flush him.

MICHAEL: Do you want to be flushed when you're dead?

NINA: I'm never going to die.

MICHAEL: Help me find a box!

NINA: OK, OK.

MICHAEL: Maybe he was too lonely. Next time I'll ask Dad for two fish. And a turtle.

Questions

1. How long do goldfish live?

2. Are fish good or bad pets? Why?

3. If you had a pet that died, how would you feel? What would you do?

4. Where do pets go after they die?

5. Would you bury Rajah or flush him? Why?

6. Do fish have emotions? Do they feel happy and sad?

7. What's the best kind of pet and why?

8. Should Michael get more fish? Why or why not?

9. What happened to Rajah? Why do you think he died?

10. Do you believe in heaven? What do you think it's like?

TWO STEPS AHEAD

Mark has to go shopping with his mom.

Characters

Mom
Mark
Hal
Mother

(MARK takes a few steps away from MOM.)

MOM: Mark, where are you going?

MARK: Nowhere!

MOM: Don't get ahead of me. We're in the mall.
This is not the safest place.

MARK: OK!

(MARK takes a few more steps away.)

MOM: Mark, come stand by me please while I look
in this store.

MARK: I'm right here.

MOM: Yes, and I want you to stand closer to me.

(MARK takes one step toward MOM.)

MARK: There, OK?

MOM: No, not OK. Come stand next to me, Mark.

I don't want to ask you again!

MARK: Mom, we're in a ladies' store. With girl stuff.

MOM: And?

MARK: And I don't want anyone to see me here.

MOM: Well, you are here.

MARK: Can't I just stand over here?

MOM: What difference does it make if you stand over there or next to me?

MARK: I don't know.

MOM: Everyone knows you have a mother. Don't be silly. Now come where I can see you.

MARK: Mooooom, this is embarrassing!

MOM: It's embarrassing to have a mother. I'm sorry; I don't understand. Many, many people have mothers.

MARK: I hate this.

MOM: I don't care. Now come here!

(MARK *sighs and grumbles and walks over to his mother.*)

MARK: Are you happy now?

MOM: I'm very happy now.

MARK: Yuck.

MOM: That's enough, Mark.

(HAL and MOTHER enter.)

HAL: Mom, can I go to the arcade?

MOTHER: No, you have to stay with me.

HAL: Why?

MOTHER: Because it's not safe to go off alone. Maybe we can go later.

HAL: But I want to go now.

(HAL and MOTHER see MARK and MOM.)

MOTHER: Linda, it's so good to see you!

MOM: Patty, I love that sweater! You look great!

MOTHER: Thank you! See anything nice here today?

MOM: There's a great sale going on.

HAL: Hey.

MARK: Hey.

(HAL and MARK stand around for a minute, looking embarrassed.)

MARK: This is stupid. My mom made me come.

HAL: Me, too. I wanted to go to the arcade and play video games.

MARK: That would be way better.

HAL: Can Mark and me go to the arcade together?

MOTHER: Mark and I. Can Mark and I go to the arcade together.

HAL: Well, can we?

MOTHER: No, we have to stick together.

MARK: Please, Mom?

MOM: No, you heard what Mrs. O'Keefe said. We have to stick together.

MARK: I hate shopping.

HAL: Me, too.

Questions

1. Why do the boys' mothers want them to stay nearby?

2. How can places like the mall be dangerous?

3. Are the mothers right not to let Mark and Hal go to the arcade together?

4. Is it embarrassing to spend time with your mother in public? Why or why not?

5. Why are boys sometimes embarrassed to be around girls, even their mothers?

6. Do you like being cared for and protected or would you rather have more freedom?

7. Why do some boys hate shopping?

PAINT HOG

John is painting a masterpiece—and hogging the blue paint!

Characters

Eric
John
Victoria

(An art class. JOHN is painting with a lot of tubes of paint around him. ERIC is next to him.)

ERIC: John, can I have the blue?

JOHN: No, I'm using it.

ERIC: But I need it.

JOHN: But I'm using it.

ERIC: Can I just have some and give it back to you?

JOHN: No, I'm using it now.

ERIC: No, you're not. You're using red.

JOHN: But I'm using the blue next. I need it.

ERIC: Fine. I'll use green.

(VICTORIA enters.)

VICTORIA: John, can I have the blue?

JOHN: No, I'm using it.

VICTORIA: Well, you can't hog it.

JOHN: I'm using it!

VICTORIA: It's the only one left. You can't keep it to yourself.

JOHN: Alexandra has another blue one.

VICTORIA: That one is dried out. We can't get anything out of it.

JOHN: Too bad.

VICTORIA: You can't hog it, John!

JOHN: Go find another.

VICTORIA: Nope. I'm going to take this one.

(VICTORIA reaches across JOHN and takes the blue paint.)

JOHN: Give it back!

VICTORIA: When I'm done!

JOHN: I need it now!

VICTORIA: You have to wait.

(VICTORIA starts to paint on the other side of ERIC.)

ERIC: Good. John is such a paint hog.

JOHN: I can hear you!

ERIC: Well, you are. So, Victoria, can I have the blue?

VICTORIA: No. I'm using it.

ERIC: Can we share?

VICTORIA: No. I'm doing something important.

ERIC: I really need the blue. I haven't been able to use it all day.

VICTORIA: When I'm done, you can have it.

JOHN: Nope. I get it when you're done. Remember?

VICTORIA: You get it after John is done.

ERIC: But John is never done!

VICTORIA: Eric, you have to be patient and wait your turn!

ERIC: I've been waiting ALL DAY!

Questions

1. What should Eric do?

2. Is Victoria being fair?

3. Do you like sharing or hate sharing?

4. Do you know anyone who hogs toys or art supplies?

5. How does it make you feel when someone won't share with you?

6. Should Eric have gotten the blue paint before Victoria?

GORILLA MY DREAMS

Robin wants the same toys as the other kids in school.

Characters

Robin
Mom

ROBIN: Mom! Mom! Can I talk to you?

MOM: What is it, Robin? Are you OK?

ROBIN: I'm OK. I just want to talk to you!

MOM: OK, OK! Calm down! Now what is it?

ROBIN: Mom, this is very important. Are you listening?

MOM: Yes, I'm listening.

ROBIN: OK. I want—I need the Girly Gorilla Gang.

MOM: What?

ROBIN: Listen, Mom! I need the Girly Gorilla Gang.

MOM: What is the Girly Gorilla Gang?

ROBIN: Moooom, the Girly Gorilla Gang are these cute toys that everybody has at school, and I need them a lot!

MOM: Why do you need them?

ROBIN: Because everyone in school has them,
like I said.

MOM: If everyone in school has them, can't you
just play with their Girly Gorillas?

ROBIN: It's the Girly Gorilla Gang, Mom. And no,
I can't play with theirs. I need my own.

MOM: Well, how much are they?

ROBIN: I think they're about thirty dollars each,
and there are twelve of them.

MOM: That's a lot of money!

ROBIN: I know, but it's important.

MOM: It's important that we eat and have a roof
over our heads! It is not important for you to
have some gorillas.

ROBIN: I told you, Mom, that it's the Girly—

MOM: —Gorilla Gang! I heard you! But you cannot
have them.

ROBIN: Why not?

MOM: Now you're not listening. We don't have the
money, Robin.

ROBIN: Can you get the money?

MOM: No.

ROBIN: Why not?

MOM: It's impossible. And if I got extra money, I would spend it on more important things.

ROBIN: But, Mom, this is—

MOM: You're not getting those new toys, Robin. And that's that.

ROBIN: You don't love me.

MOM: I do so love you. You know I love you.

ROBIN: No, you don't. If you loved me, you'd buy me the Girly Gorilla Gang.

MOM: Robin, you're not being nice. I love you, but you are not getting those toys. Let's not talk any more about this!

ROBIN: Oh, Mommy, pleeeeeeeease?

MOM: No. That's enough.

ROBIN: I hate you!

(ROBIN runs away.)

MOM: Do you think you're going to get any toys with that attitude, young lady?

Questions

1. Is Robin's mom being mean?

2. Is Robin being mean to her mom?

3. Should you be able to get a toy if other kids have it?

4. Do you think Robin will ever get the Girly Gorilla Gang?

5. Do you think the reason Robin's mom gave her (not enough money) is a good reason not to get the toys?

6. Why do parents sometimes get mad when you beg for something you want?

7. Does Robin hate her mom?

8. Does Robin's mom not love her?

THE MOVIE

Liam has to go to the movies with his sister, Natalie.

Characters

Mom
Natalie
Liam

MOM: Natalie!

(*NATALIE enters.*)

NATALIE: Yes, Mom?

MOM: I want you to baby-sit your brother for a few hours.

NATALIE: I can't!

MOM: You can't?

NATALIE: I promised Ellen I would go to the movies with her.

MOM: You need to cancel your plans.

NATALIE: Mom, I can't!

MOM: I'm sorry, Natalie. I promise you will get to go to the movies with Ellen another day.

NATALIE: But I promised her, Mom!

MOM: I'm sorry, but I have to go to work.

NATALIE: Can you work another day?

MOM: No, this is important. Please do this for me, Natalie. I wouldn't ask you if it was not important.

NATALIE: Yuck. I don't want to watch Liam. I feel like I'm always baby-sitting him.

MOM: Liam!

LIAM: *(Yelling from offstage.)* What, Mom?

MOM: Come here, Liam!

LIAM: What?

MOM: Liam, come down here and talk to me!

(A moment of silence.)

LIAM: I'm watching cartoons!

MOM: Liam, get down here now!

LIAM: OoooooK.

NATALIE: Mom, I just got an idea!

MOM: What?

NATALIE: Can I take Liam with me to the movies?

MOM: Well . . .

NATALIE: I promise we will take really good care of him. He might like it.

MOM: Well . . . OK. I suppose that will be all right as long as an adult is driving.

NATALIE: I know Ellen's father will drive us. No problem.

MOM: And you won't let Liam out of your sight?

NATALIE: No. Promise.

MOM: Well, OK.

(LIAM enters.)

MOM: OK, Liam, I have to go in to work. Your sister will be in charge.

LIAM: Do you have to?

MOM: It will be fine. You two have a good time. I'll see you soon!

(MOM exits.)

LIAM: Aw, yuck. You better not be bossy.

NATALIE: Come on, Liam, we're going to the movies.

LIAM: We are!

NATALIE: Yes.

LIAM: Yay! What are we going to see?

NATALIE: *Love Forever.*

LIAM: What?!

NATALIE: *Love Forever.*

LIAM: That's a girl's movie.

NATALIE: Let's go.

LIAM: I don't want to go!

NATALIE: Mom says I'm in charge. Now let's go!

LIAM: I want to see *Fire Swamp*!

NATALIE: You can't. Look, it's bad enough that I have to spend my day with my baby brother! Don't make this any harder. Let's go.

LIAM: I'm telling Mom. This stinks!

NATALIE: I know!

Questions

1. What movie do you think Liam and Natalie will see?

2. Do you think it's fair for Liam to have to go to the movies with Natalie?

3. Do you think it's fair for Natalie to have to baby-sit Liam?

4. Should Mom have stayed home from work?

5. Who do you think is more upset—Liam or Natalie?

6. Why do older brothers and sisters sometimes not want to spend time with younger brothers and sisters?

7. Why do kids usually hang around with other kids their age?

MISS ROCKIN' ROBOTS

Gwen wants to play Rockin' Robots with the boys.

Characters
Peter
Becket
Gwen
Joy

PETER: I am gonna crush you!

BECKET: You are not.

PETER: You wait and see. I've never lost Rockin' Robots.

BECKET: Sure you have. I beat you last week.

PETER: No, you didn't. My mom called me, and I got distracted. That doesn't count.

(GWEN enters.)

GWEN: Did I hear you talk about the Rockin' Robots game?

BECKET: Yeah.

GWEN: I love that game! Can I play it with you? I'm really good.

PETER: No, you can't, and no, you're not.

GWEN: What?

PETER: You can't play with us, and you are not good at it.

GWEN: Sure I am. How do you know?

BECKET: 'Cause you're a girl.

GWEN: And you're a boy. So what?

BECKET: So Rockin' Robots is a boy game.

GWEN: No, it's not.

PETER: There are two boys playing it on the box.

BECKET: Right! And robots are guy stuff. You should go play dolls with the girls.

GWEN: I don't like dolls.

PETER: Maybe she's not a girl.

GWEN: I'm a girl!

BECKET: Girls do girl stuff, boys do boy stuff.

GWEN: That's not fair! And it's wrong. I should get to play whatever I want!

PETER: Hey, Joy!

(JOY enters.)

JOY: What is it, stink-face?

PETER: Do girls like to play with dolls?

JOY: Yes. Of course.

BECKET: And do girls like to play Rockin' Robots?

JOY: No.

GWEN: I do.

JOY: You do?

GWEN: It's fun. You punch the other robot until he falls right over.

JOY: But the boys always punch the buttons until the game breaks.

GWEN: You have to punch the buttons! That's how you play.

JOY: Yuck.

GWEN: Try it. Play with me.

JOY: No, thanks.

GWEN: I promise I won't punch the buttons.

JOY: No. I'm playing Barbies with Joanna and Britney.

GWEN: Oh.

BECKET: See?

PETER: We were right.

GWEN: Well, I think you're wrong.

BECKET: Too bad.

GWEN: Guess what?

PETER/BECKET: What?

GWEN: You don't have the game.

PETER: Yeah, it's over there.

GWEN: First one who gets it, gets to play!

(PETER and GWEN run offstage.)

BECKET: No fair! That's our game!

Questions

1. Do you think it's strange for girls to want to play games boys like? Why?

2. Do you think it's strange for boys to want to play games girls like? Why?

3. Do you prefer to play with boys or girls? Why?

4. Do you think Gwen should be allowed to play the Rockin' Robots game?

5. Should Peter and Becket play with her?

6. Why do girls play with girls and boys play with boys a lot of the time?

SOCKS FOR CHRISTMAS

Carl gets socks for Christmas, and he is not happy about it!

Characters

Mom
Ezra
Carl
Juliet
Aunt Rochelle

(CARL, EZRA, and JULIET, MOM, and AUNT ROCHELLE enter a room with a sofa and a Christmas tree with a few presents underneath it.)

MOM: Ooooo, look, kids! There are presents under the tree!

EZRA: Presents!

CARL: I hope I got a Max Power action figures set.

JULIET: Can we open them?

AUNT ROCHELLE: Yes, you can open them! They are for you!

EZRA: Yeah, Santa!

MOM: These presents are from Aunt Rochelle.

JULIET: *(Opening one present.)* I got a little doll! She's pretty.

MOM: What do you say to Aunt Rochelle?

JULIET: Thank you!

EZRA: *(Opening one present.)* I got a fire truck! Thank you, Aunt Rochelle!

CARL: *(Opening one present.)* I got . . . socks. *(He stands up and throws the socks across the room.)* I hate socks!

MOM: Carl! Behave yourself! What do you say to Aunt Rochelle?

CARL: *(Crossing his arms in front of him.)* Nothing!

MOM: Carl! That is not how we behave! You say thank you to Aunt Rochelle.

CARL: I hate socks! Juliet got a doll and Ezra got a fire truck and I got socks? This stinks!

MOM: Now, Carl, you need socks. You are always getting holes in your socks.

EZRA: I like socks. I have socks with fire trucks on them.

AUNT ROCHELLE: They sound nice, Ezra!

CARL: Well, I hate socks.

MOM: Carl, you come over here this instant and apologize to Aunt Rochelle! She picked out those socks especially for you. I want you to say thank you and behave like a nice boy!

AUNT ROCHELLE: It's OK. Carl, why don't you open your other present?

MOM: No. Carl is not going to open any more presents until he can apologize and say thank you like a polite, nice boy.

CARL: I don't care! I don't want any more presents! This stinks!

MOM: Carl, you go pick up those socks right now.

CARL: Fine.

(CARL picks up the socks.)

MOM: Now come here, Carl.

(CARL goes over to MOM. MOM whispers in CARL's ear.)

JULIET: My doll has a pretty face. I'm going to call her Tanisha. That's the name of my best friend in school.

AUNT ROCHELLE: That's wonderful, Juliet! What a beautiful name.

(CARL walks over to AUNT ROCHELLE.)

CARL: *(Looking down at his feet.)* I'm sorry, Aunt Rochelle. Thank you for the socks.

MOM: That's better, Carl. Now you can open another present.

EZRA: Can I open another present?

JULIET: And can I open another present?

AUNT ROCHELLE: Everyone can open another present!

(CARL, EZRA, and JULIET each open another present.)

EZRA: Socks! I love socks!

CARL: Two Max Power action figures! Thank you, Aunt Rochelle!

JULIET: A book? I hate books!

(JULIET throws the book.)

EZRA: Uh-oh.

CARL: Not again.

Questions

1. How should you behave if someone gives you a present you don't like or don't want?

2. Should Carl and Juliet apologize for their behavior?

3. Should Carl and Juliet be punished? If so, how?

4. Which kid do you think is the youngest?

5. Have you ever wished and hoped for something a lot and not gotten it? How did it make you feel? Do you still want it or did you forget about it?

6. What should you say when someone does something nice or gives you something? Why do people say thank you?

Part 5
MEAN!

What are these characters saying?
What's going on in this picture?
You decide!

THE GAME

Rachel and Paul are picking people for their teams. Who will pick Amy the Klutz?

Characters

Rachel
Paul
Amy
Jonas

(NOTE: You can also have people playing the other children picked, if you are performing this scene onstage.)

RACHEL: I'll take Jonas.

PAUL: Hey, I wanted him on my team!

RACHEL: It was my turn.

PAUL: You knew I wanted him on my team.

RACHEL: That's the rules. Now it's your turn to pick.

PAUL: I guess I'll take Henry.

RACHEL: I'll take . . . Olivia.

PAUL: I'll take Rose.

RACHEL: David, come on down!

PAUL: I'll take Chris.

RACHEL: I'll take Kristy.

PAUL: I'll take . . .

RACHEL: You have to pick a girl next.

PAUL: I'll take Tara.

RACHEL: Amy.

AMY: What?

RACHEL: You're on my team.

JONAS: What?! She's the worst one! Why did you pick the worst one!

PAUL: I'll take Brendan.

JONAS: You could have picked a boy! It was the turn to pick a boy!

RACHEL: So?

JONAS: You picked Amy! She's the worst player ever! No, wait, Paul. We need to do a do-over.

PAUL: You can't. You already picked.

JONAS: No, we need to do it again.

RACHEL: No, we don't.

JONAS: Yes, we do!

RACHEL: I'm the leader of this team, not you.

JONAS: Well, it should be me. You made a terrible decision.

RACHEL: I want Amy on our team.

AMY: Oh . . . thanks. But I'm not very good.

RACHEL: Sure you are. You're fine.

JONAS: No, she's not. She stinks. We're going to lose!

RACHEL: Jonas, do you think you're really good?

JONAS: I know I'm really good. I'm the best player. That's why you picked me first, remember?

RACHEL: Well, if you're so good, it shouldn't matter if there are people on our team who are . . . not as good.

JONAS: Amy isn't "not as good," she's terrible. The only time she ever scored, she made a goal for the other team. She can't throw, she can't catch, she can't do anything! She just gets in the way! Do you want to win or not?

RACHEL: Jonas, it's just a game. Let's keep going. I pick . . .

JONAS: No, wait. We have to do a do-over.

PAUL: You already picked.

RACHEL: I already picked.

PAUL: You can't do a do-over.

RACHEL: I don't want to do a do-over. Let's keep going.

AMY: Maybe I should just go back. So we don't fight.

RACHEL: No, Amy. Stay where you are.

JONAS: Good idea. Go away, Amy.

RACHEL: Don't be mean, Jonas!

AMY: I'm not feeling that good anyway.

RACHEL: Of course you're not. Jonah's being very mean. But don't worry about him.

AMY: I think I should sit down.

RACHEL: Don't be silly. It's just a game. I pick Jill.

PAUL: I pick Laura.

RACHEL: OK, let's play!

JONAS: Paul, can we swap Laura for Amy?

PAUL: No way!

AMY: I'm sick. I need to sit down.

RACHEL: Come on; let's just play!

AMY: I don't think I want to play anymore.

(AMY walks away.)

RACHEL: See what you did, Jonas?

JONAS: Yeah, maybe we'll win now!

Questions

1. Who do you agree with—Jonas or Rachel?

2. Have you ever been picked last for a team? What do you think that feels like?

3. Why do you think Amy chooses not to play?

4. Which is more important when you play a game—winning or having a good time?

5. What do you think Rachel's personality is like?

6. Do you think being a good athlete is something you learn or something you're born with?

7. Is being a good sport part of being a good athlete?

BABY SISTER

Sure, Mike will play with his baby sister—if she does exactly what he wants her to do!

Characters
Mike
Erin
Mom

MIKE: Erin, let's play a game.

ERIN: Yay!

MIKE: OK, when the mailman comes, I want you to pretend you're a puppy and get the mail in your teeth.

ERIN: No!

MIKE: Why not?

ERIN: I don't want to do that in front of the mailman!

MIKE: Why not?

ERIN: He'll laugh at me!

MIKE: So?

ERIN: So?

MIKE: He won't laugh at you.

ERIN: He will!

MIKE: So what? It'll be funny. Come on, Erin. You always say you want me to play with you. If you don't do this, I'll never play with you again.

ERIN: That's mean.

MIKE: No, it'll be fun! You get to pretend to be a little puppy! Come on, Erin; do it!

ERIN: Well . . .

MIKE: It will be fun . . .

ERIN: Will you play house with me afterwards?

MIKE: Maybe.

ERIN: Maybe? You have to say yes, Mike.

MIKE: I might not have time. I have to do my homework.

ERIN: No, you don't. You told Dad you did your homework.

MIKE: I just said that so I could watch TV. I still have to do my homework. Now, are you going to bark like a dog, crawl on the floor, and get the mail in your teeth or not?

ERIN: I don't know.

MIKE: Let's play doggie! Come on! I'll put some cookies in a bowl and you can eat them like a puppy.

ERIN: Then we can play house? I'll be the mom, and you can be the baby.

MIKE: I'm not going to be the baby.

ERIN: You can be the dad then.

(MOM enters. MIKE and ERIN don't see her.)

MIKE: The mailman is coming! Quick! Crawl out on the porch and bark at him! I'll open the door so you can get the mail in your teeth.

MOM: What?

MIKE: Hi, Mom. Erin is going to get the mail. Excuse us.

MOM: Wait a minute. What's all this about getting the mail in her teeth?

MIKE: We're playing doggie. If you want, she can get your slippers in your teeth and bring them to you.

MOM: Is this OK with you, Erin?

ERIN: Mike said if I do this, he'll play house with me.

MIKE: Maybe. Just maybe.

MOM: I don't know about this, Mike. I think you're taking advantage of your sister's good humor.

MIKE: What does that mean?

MOM: You're having fun at her expense.

ERIN: What does that mean?

MOM: He's making you do something he wouldn't do himself.

MIKE: I might pretend to be a dog. If I were younger, like Erin.

MOM: But you wouldn't now—

MIKE: The mailman's at the door! Come on, do it, Erin! It will be cute, Mom!

MOM: Mike, are you done your homework?

MIKE: Yes—

ERIN: No, he's not. He said he told Dad he was so he could watch TV, but he wasn't.

MOM: Mike, go do your homework.

MIKE: Thanks a lot, Erin!

ERIN: Can we play house later, Mike?

MIKE: No way!

MOM: Mike, talk nicely to your sister.

Questions

1. Was Mike making fun of his sister or just playing with her?

2. Should Erin have gone along with Mike's plan? Why or why not?

3. Would Mike have played house with Erin later?

4. How do you think the mailman would react if Erin pretended to be a puppy?

5. Was the mom right to stop Mike's plan?

6. Should Erin have tattled on Mike?

7. Should anyone be punished?

8. How can you tell that Mike is older than Erin?

TURKEY FACE

Jenna and Lea are calling Emma names.
What will happen next?

Characters

Jenna
Emma
Lea
Aaron
Tom

(JENNA and LEA are onstage.)

JENNA: Hey, Emma, come over here!

(EMMA enters.)

EMMA: Hi!

LEA: You got your hair cut.

EMMA: Do you like it?

JENNA: You look like you have a skunk on your head.

EMMA: What?

LEA: You look like you have a skunk on your head.

EMMA: Why?

JENNA: You just do.

EMMA: But it's not black and white like a skunk.

LEA: You're the Lady with the Skunk in Her Hair.

EMMA: I am not.

JENNA: You are too. That's your new name.

LEA: Lady with the Skunk in Her Hair!

EMMA: Stop it!

JENNA: Make us!

EMMA: That's mean.

LEA: No, it's not. It's the truth.

EMMA: That I have a skunk on my head? That's not the truth. Take it back!

(AARON and TOM enter.)

AARON: What's going on?

LEA: Emma is the Lady with the Skunk in Her Hair!

EMMA: I am not!

TOM: What are you talking about?

EMMA: See? I do not look like I have a skunk in my hair.

JENNA: Yes, you do! I can see the skunk. Hello, skunk!

EMMA: Stop it! Well, at least I didn't get an F on the last math test!

JENNA: How did you know that?

EMMA: I saw your grade. You got an F. You're stupid in math.

LEA: No, she's not.

EMMA: Yes, she is. I saw her grade.

LEA: You shouldn't look at other people's papers. I'm telling the teacher.

EMMA: Then I'll tell her that you're calling me names.

LEA: But you are the Lady with the Skunk in Her Hair!

EMMA: And Jenna is stupid in math!

(JENNA runs away.)

LEA: See? You made her cry. You're mean, Emma.

EMMA: I'm mean?

LEA: You're mean!

(LEA exits.)

EMMA: That didn't make any sense!

TOM: Wow.

AARON: Girls are mean.

EMMA: I wasn't mean! They were mean!

AARON: When we get mad at someone, we just punch them.

TOM: Yeah, then we're friends again.

AARON: Girls are mean!

EMMA: I didn't do anything!

TOM: Let's get out of here, Turkey Face.

AARON: *(Kidding.)* You called me a name! I'm gonna cry.

(TOM and AARON exit, laughing.)

EMMA: I didn't do anything! I was nice! They started it!

Questions

1. Who was meaner—Jenna and Lea or Emma?

2. Is it meaner to say something true or to say a lie about someone?

3. Do boys and girls fight differently? How?

4. What would you do if you were Emma and the other girls called you the Lady with the Skunk in Her Hair?

5. Why do people call each other names?

6. Why do you think Jenna and Lea decided to pick on Emma?

7. If Lea tells the teacher that Emma saw Jenna's math grade, will Emma get in trouble?

8. If Emma tells the teacher that Jenna and Lea were calling her names, will Jenna and Lea get in trouble?

HOWDY, PARTNER

Joel doesn't like his partner in gym class.

Characters

Coach Adams
Joel
Christopher
Nick
Bill

COACH ADAMS: OK, everybody! Find a partner.

JOEL: Christopher, be my partner!

CHRISTOPHER: I can't! I told Bill I'd be his partner.

JOEL: Who needs a partner?

NICK: I do.

JOEL: Oh. Anybody else need a partner?

COACH ADAMS: Joel, you and Nick are partners.

JOEL: But I don't want to be his partner.

COACH ADAMS: No arguing. Let's go, boys. One guy needs to hold the other guy's feet. We're taking turns doing sit-ups.

(CHRISTOPHER holds BILL's feet down. BILL starts doing sit-ups.)

JOEL: Coach? I don't want to be Nick's partner.

COACH ADAMS: I heard you. But you are Nick's partner.

JOEL: But I don't want to be his partner.

COACH ADAMS: I heard you, Mr. Holiday, but you are Nick's partner, so go hold his feet so we can do some sit-ups!

JOEL: Coach, his feet smell.

COACH ADAMS: I've had enough of this silly stuff. There's nothing wrong with Mr. Pastorelli. Stop arguing and get moving!

JOEL: Fine.

(JOEL walks over to NICK. NICK and JOEL both sit on the ground.)

JOEL: Fine. I guess I'm your partner. But I don't want to be.

NICK: OK.

CHRISTOPHER: Hey, what's your problem, Joel?

JOEL: I have to be Nick's partner.

CHRISTOPHER: So what?

JOEL: It's Nick, Christopher. Icky Nicky. Nick the Hick. Smelly Pastorelli!

CHRISTOPHER: Get over it.

JOEL: Why don't you be his partner then?

CHRISTOPHER: Because I'm Bill's partner. Duh.

JOEL: Hey, Bill!

(BILL stops doing sit-ups.)

BILL: No!

JOEL: No what?

BILL: No, I won't be Nick's partner.

JOEL: How did you know—

BILL: I have ears, Joel. I heard you talking about it.

JOEL: Well, then, I'll be your partner, and Christopher can be Nick's partner, since he doesn't mind.

CHRISTOPHER: We're already partners.

JOEL: You told me to "get over it," so why don't you be Nick's partner.

CHRISTOPHER: OK, fine! It's not a big deal! Come on, Nick. Sit-ups.

(CHRISTOPHER holds NICK's feet. NICK does sit-ups.)

JOEL: That's better.

BILL: It's your turn. I already went.

CHRISTOPHER: You're such a dummy, Joel.

JOEL: Takes one to know one.

Questions

1. How do you think Nick feels?

2. Why doesn't Nick say anything in his defense?

3. Is Joel being mean?

4. You don't always get to work with or sit next to your friends at school. How should you act around people you don't like as much?

5. Why do some kids get picked on more than others?

6. What can you do to stop bullies and name-callers?

7. What could Coach Adams do to make things better between the boys?

BACK OFF, BRANDY

Brandy wants Robert to play house with her.
Robert wants Brandy to leave him alone.

Characters
Brandy
Robert
Frank
Elizabeth
Mrs. Prentiss

BRANDY: Robert, we're playing house. I'm the mom, and you're the dad.

ROBERT: I don't want to play.

BRANDY: You have to.

ROBERT: No, I don't.

BRANDY: But you're the only one who can play the dad.

ROBERT: Why?

BRANDY: Because we're going to get married.

ROBERT: No, we're not!

BRANDY: Yes, we are.

ROBERT: No, we're not! I don't like you, Brandy. I'm not marrying anybody.

BRANDY: Yes, you are. Everybody gets married.

ROBERT: No, they don't. My Uncle Keith never got married. He rides a motorcycle.

BRANDY: I don't care about your uncle. Now you are the dad, and I am the mom, and Elizabeth is the sister who is seven, and Frank is the baby.

FRANK: I don't want to be a baby.

BRANDY: You are the baby! Now go take a nap over there.

FRANK: OK.

(FRANK walks over to the corner and lies down.)

ELIZABETH: Daddy, I hurt my finger!

ROBERT: I'm not playing!

ELIZABETH: Daddy, can I have a Band-Aid?

ROBERT: No. Leave me alone. I'm not playing with you guys.

BRANDY: Come here, Sally. That's your name, OK, Elizabeth?

ELIZABETH: OK.

BRANDY: Come here, Sally. I'll bandage your finger.

(ELIZABETH walks over to BRANDY who pretends to put a Band-Aid on ELIZABETH's finger.)

BRANDY: Now go to bed, Sally.

ELIZABETH: OK, Mommy.

(ELIZABETH walks over to another corner and lies down.)

BRANDY: How was your day at work, husband?

ROBERT: I'm not your husband. I'm not playing!

BRANDY: Yes, you are. We're going to get married.

ROBERT: I don't want to marry you! Go away!

(ROBERT pushes BRANDY away. [IMPORTANT NOTE: In plays, no one ever gets pushed or hit or hurt for real. It's all pretend!] MRS. PRENTISS enters.)

MRS. PRENTISS: Robert! Did I just see you push Brandy?

ROBERT: She was bothering me.

MRS. PRENTISS: Is it ever OK to push someone?

ROBERT: She thinks I'm going to marry her. I don't want to marry her! I told her a hundred times.

MRS. PRENTISS: Robert, go inside for the rest of recess. Pushing and shoving is never allowed at school!

ROBERT: But she wouldn't stop bothering me!

MRS. PRENTISS: There is no excuse for violent behavior. Brandy, you and Robert are not to play together again.

ROBERT: Good!

MRS. PRENTISS: Robert, go inside immediately!

Questions

1. Why did Robert push Brandy? Can you understand why he did it?

2. Was it wrong for Robert to push Brandy?

3. Robert told Brandy to leave him alone and that he didn't want to play. What else could Robert do to get Brandy to stop bothering him?

4. Was what Mrs. Prentiss did right? Why did she punish Robert and not Brandy? Is that fair?

5. Pushing and hitting can hurt people. Can words hurt people? How?

6. Was Robert trying to hurt Brandy?

CANDY DAY

*Candy thinks Halloween is her special day.
Does that mean she should get more treats
than everyone else?*

Characters

Candy
Rebecca
Jonah
Mrs. Pollard
Mr. Hardy

*(JONAH is dressed in a vampire costume.
CANDY is dressed as a princess. REBECCA is
dressed as a baseball player. It is Halloween.
They are standing outside of REBECCA's house.)*

CANDY: It's my favorite day of the year! It's my day!

REBECCA: Candy, it's Halloween.

CANDY: Exactly. Halloween is Candy Day, and I
am Candy!

JONAH: You are weird.

REBECCA: Takes one to know one.

JONAH: Why are you taking her side?

(MRS. POLLARD—Rebecca's mom—enters.)

MRS. POLLARD: OK, everybody ready to go?

JONAH: Yeah!

REBECCA: Let's go, Mom!

CANDY: Mrs. Pollard, today is my day!

MRS. POLLARD: Is that right?

CANDY: Yes!

MRS. POLLARD: Why is today your day, Candy?

CANDY: Because everyone gives out candy, so it's Candy Day, and my name is Candy!

MRS. POLLARD: Oh, I guess you're right! All set? Does everybody have a bag to hold their candy?

JONAH: Yes! Can we please go now, Mrs. Pollard?

MRS. POLLARD: Yes, let's go. Let's start next door at Mr. Hardy's house.

(REBECCA, JONAH, CANDY, and MRS. POL-LARD walk up to MR. HARDY's door.)

MRS. POLLARD: Who is going to ring the doorbell?

JONAH: Me! Me! I mean, me, please, Mrs. Pollard.

MRS. POLLARD: OK, Jonah, ring the doorbell.

REBECCA: Wait! We have to say "Trick or Treat" all together. OK?

CANDY: I want to say "Candy Day"!

REBECCA: You have to say "Trick or Treat," Candy.

JONAH: Yeah, it's the rules.

MRS. POLLARD: It's the tradition!

REBECCA: OK, ready?

CANDY: I'm scared.

MRS. POLLARD: Everything will be fine, Candy. Jonah, ring the doorbell.

(JONAH rings the doorbell. MR. HARDY opens the door.)

JONAH/REBECCA/CANDY: Trick or Treat!

CANDY: Candy Day!

REBECCA: Candy! Don't say that!

MR. HARDY: Well, I think I prefer Treat to Trick. After all, it is Candy Day.

CANDY: See? I told you, Rebecca.

MR. HARDY: Now what have we here? A vampire—my! you're scary!—a famous baseball player and a queen—

CANDY: No, I'm a princess.

MR. HARDY: Of course you are! Everyone take a piece of candy.

(MR. HARDY *holds out a big bowl of candy.* REBECCA *takes a piece, Jonah takes a piece, and* CANDY *takes two big handfuls.*)

MRS. POLLARD: Candy, you shouldn't take so much. Mr. Hardy needs enough candy for all the children in the neighborhood.

REBECCA: Yeah, Candy, you're being greedy!

JONAH: That's against the rules.

CANDY: But it's my day! My name is Candy—

JONAH: It is not your day, Candy. You made that up.

CANDY: It is, too!

REBECCA: No, Candy. It's Halloween. People just give away candy on Halloween. It has nothing to do with you.

CANDY: Yes, it does!

MRS. POLLARD: Candy, Mr. Hardy told you to take a piece. Why don't you choose one piece of candy and give back the rest?

MR. HARDY: Oh, it's OK.

MRS. POLLARD: Mr. Hardy, we don't want you to run out of candy. We need to be fair.

CANDY: I want to go home now.

MRS. POLLARD: But, Candy, we have a lot more houses to visit. I bet if you take one piece of candy from all of those houses, you'll have quite a lot of candy!

CANDY: No. I want to go home.

MR. HARDY: It's OK. She can keep the candy.

REBECCA: Come on, Candy! Give back the extra and let's keep going.

JONAH: Yeah, I want to go to every house.

CANDY: No. I don't like this anymore. I want to go home.

MRS. POLLARD: Come on, Candy. Everything's fine. Now give back the extra candy to Mr. Hardy, and we will go to the next house.

CANDY: You're not my mother.

MRS. POLLARD: I bet your mother would tell you the same thing. Come on, let's go.

MR. HARDY: You sure look pretty, little princess!

JONAH: Come on, Candy!

CANDY: Fine!

(CANDY *dumps the candy back into MR. HARDY's bowl and just takes one piece back, putting it in her bag.*)

MRS. POLLARD: Good! Let's go see Miss Marianne now! Oooo, look! She has a spider web on her front door!

JONAH: Cool!

CANDY: I'm scared. I want to go home.

JONAH: Don't be a sissy, Candy.

REBECCA: Don't you want more candy?

MRS. POLLARD: Everything is going to be fine. Who is going to ring this doorbell?

REBECCA: I will!

CANDY: I don't like Halloween.

Questions

1. Why does Candy think Halloween is her day?

2. Why does Mrs. Pollard tell Candy to give back the handfuls of treats that she took from Mr. Hardy's bowl?

3. Do you think Candy should have given the treats back to Mr. Hardy? Why or why not?

4. Why do children say "Trick or Treat" on Halloween?

5. How do you decide what to wear on Halloween?

6. Do you think Candy will go back home or do you think Candy will keep Trick or Treating?

7. What if Candy got to keep all the treats she took from Mr. Hardy? Does that mean all the children should get more candy? How would the other children feel if only Candy got a lot of extra candy?

8. What does it mean to be greedy? Is Candy greedy?

9. Do you find Halloween scary? Why or why not?

NOT INVITED

Audrey isn't invited to Eve's birthday party.

Characters
Dana
Audrey
Marina
Clay
Quint
Eve

DANA: I'm so excited about the party!

AUDREY: What party?

DANA: Eve's party!

AUDREY: Eve is having a party?

DANA: Didn't you get invited?

AUDREY: I . . . did. I mean . . . I think I did.

MARINA: I bet you did. Everybody in the class got invited.

AUDREY: I don't remember. Maybe—I bet my mom has the invitation.

DANA: That's probably it.

MARINA: Yeah.

(DANA, AUDREY, and MARINA stand quietly for a minute. AUDREY is thinking.)

AUDREY: You guys . . . what if I didn't get an invitation?

MARINA: I bet you did. I bet your mom just has it.

DANA: Or maybe you forgot.

AUDREY: I don't think I got one.

MARINA: Really?

AUDREY: Everyone else got one?

MARINA: I think so.

DANA: Hey, Clay! Quint!

AUDREY: Don't call them over here!

MARINA: They're boys.

DANA: So? You guys! Come over here!

(CLAY and QUINT enter.)

CLAY: What do you want?

DANA: Did you get invited to Eve's party?

QUINT: Everybody in the class got invited.

CLAY: I don't think I'm going. Are you going, Quint?

QUINT: I think I have to go.

CLAY: Then I guess I'm going.

QUINT: There will be cake, right?

MARINA: It's a birthday party.

QUINT: Well, that's good.

CLAY: My mom will make me dress up. And it's a girl party.

DANA: So?

CLAY: So I'm just saying it's a girl party.

QUINT: Can we go now?

DANA: OK.

(CLAY and QUINT exit.)

AUDREY: Clay and Quint got an invitation and I didn't?

MARINA: Are you sure you didn't get an invitation?

AUDREY: I'm pretty sure. Do you think Eve hates me?

DANA: Eve doesn't hate you. Maybe your invitation got lost. Eve!

AUDREY: Don't call her over here!

DANA: Why not?

(EVE enters.)

EVE: Hi, you guys.

MARINA: Eve, did you invite Audrey to your party?

DANA: Because she doesn't think she got an invitation, and we told her probably her mom has it or it got lost in the mail.

EVE: No, I didn't invite Audrey.

AUDREY: Why?

EVE: My mom said I could only invite ten girls and ten boys.

AUDREY: So you invited Clay and Quint instead of me?

EVE: I asked my mom if I could have twenty girls instead or fifteen girls and five boys, and she said no. So I had to invite Clay and Quint and not you.

AUDREY: So you like ten other girls more than me?

EVE: You're number eleven or twelve.

AUDREY: Oh.

EVE: See you at the party, Marina and Dana!

MARINA/DANA: See you!

AUDREY: This is the worst thing ever. Eve is not my friend anymore. She's number eight billion on my list!

MARINA: Don't be mad. You almost made the list.

DANA: I bet the party won't be that fun.

AUDREY: I invited Eve to my birthday party last year. I am never, ever going to talk to her again.

MARINA: Well, if you're not going to her party, Audrey, then I'm not going!

DANA: I'm going.

MARINA: You are?

DANA: Yeah!

MARINA: Well, then I guess I'm going, too.

AUDREY: I don't have any friends! Nobody likes me.

Questions

1. Would you go to Eve's party if you were Marina or Dana?

2. How do you think Audrey feels when she finds out she was not invited to Eve's party?

3. Do you think Eve is upset that she couldn't invite Audrey?

4. Do you think Clay and Quint will enjoy the party?

5. Is it fair to only invite a few people from class to the party? Does Eve have the right to invite only her closest friends?

6. Do you think Eve and Audrey will be friends again? How could they make up?

7. Do you think Marina, Dana, and Audrey will be friends again? Should Audrey punish Dana and Marina for going to the party without her?

Part 6
ANNOYING!

What are these characters saying?
What's going on in this picture?
You decide!

A STICKY SITUATION

Amber has gum in her hair. Who put it there?
Why didn't anyone tell her before?

Characters

Holly
Amber
Caroline
Mike

HOLLY: Amber, there's gum in your hair.

AMBER: What? How did it get there?

HOLLY: Caroline put it there.

AMBER: Why?

HOLLY: I don't know. I think she thought it was
funny.

AMBER: Caroline!

CAROLINE: What?

AMBER: Did you put gum in my hair?

CAROLINE: No.

AMBER: Well, Holly says you did.

CAROLINE: Well, I didn't.

AMBER: Holly says she saw you.

CAROLINE: Well, I didn't. She's not telling the truth.

HOLLY: I thought I saw it.

CAROLINE: You didn't. I just went to go look at it. I heard that Mike put gum in your hair and I came to see.

AMBER: Mike put gum in my hair?

CAROLINE: That's what I heard.

AMBER: Mike!

HOLLY: He's so mean.

CAROLINE: I bet he thinks it's funny.

HOLLY: You thought it was funny.

CAROLINE: I did not.

HOLLY: I saw you laugh!

AMBER: That's mean, Caroline.

CAROLINE: I didn't. Besides, Mike did it.

AMBER: Mike!

MIKE: What?

AMBER: Did you put gum in my hair?

MIKE: No. Maybe. No.

AMBER: You did!

MIKE: So? It was an accident.

AMBER: It was an accident to put gum in my hair?
I don't think so!

MIKE: Why not?

AMBER: It doesn't make sense.

CAROLINE: Yeah!

HOLLY: You shouldn't laugh. It isn't funny.

MIKE: I'm not laughing.

HOLLY: You're smiling.

MIKE: So?

AMBER: You should tell me you're sorry!

CAROLINE: She might have to look like this
forever!

MIKE: No, she won't. Just cut your hair!

AMBER: Cut my hair? Do you think I'll have to cut
my hair? This is terrible. I'm telling! Where's
Miss Randall?

MIKE: Bye!

HOLLY: You get back here.

CAROLINE: He's gonna get in trouble.

AMBER: Do you think the nurse could get it out?

CAROLINE: I don't know. It's pretty stuck.

AMBER: Why didn't you tell me, Caroline, if you saw it before?

CAROLINE: I wasn't sure it was gum.

HOLLY: You thought it was funny.

CAROLINE: I did not!

Questions

1. What do you think will happen to Amber's hair?

2. Is Holly a good friend or is she a tattletale?

3. Do you think Caroline laughed at Amber's hair? Should she have told her?

4. Is Mike guilty of putting the gum in Amber's hair?

5. Should Amber tell on Mike?

6. When is tattling good and when is it bad?

7. Does Holly make things better or worse by telling Amber what she saw?

SUMMER VACATION

Anne and Stuart get in the car for a long car ride.

Characters

Dad
Mom
Stuart
Anne

(Four chairs are set up on the stage—two in front, two in back—so everyone can be seen. These chairs are the seats in the car.)

DAD: Kids, this is going to be a great vacation!

MOM: I'm excited. Are you two?

STUART: Yes, yes, yes! I can't wait to ride the roller coasters!

MOM: Remember, there are some rides you might not be tall enough to go on.

STUART: I want to go on all of them!

DAD: We'll see, champ.

ANNE: I don't like rides.

MOM: That's OK, Anne. We'll find other things for you to do.

ANNE: Why do we have to go to Wonder World every summer? I always sit on a bench holding sodas with Mom while Dad and Stuart go on the rides. It's boring.

DAD: Oh, come on, Annie! It will be fun! You'll see.

ANNE: Can I just stay home?

MOM: Of course not.

DAD: That's enough, Anne.

ANNE: I didn't do anything!

(It is quiet for a moment. STUART pokes ANNE.)

ANNE: Ow! Stuart poked me!

STUART: No, I didn't.

(STUART pokes ANNE again.)

ANNE: Ow! He did it again!

DAD: Kids, let's behave back there.

(STUART pokes ANNE again.)

ANNE: He did it again. Stuart is poking me. Aren't you—

(STUART pokes ANNE again.)

ANNE: —going to do anything about it?

MOM: Stuaaaart . . . be good . . .

STUART: I'm not doing anything.

ANNE: Yes, you are. You're poking me.

STUART: No, I'm not. Am I poking you now?

ANNE: No, but you were.

STUART: So? You're not hurt.

ANNE: So, you shouldn't poke anyone ever!

STUART: Don't be a baby.

ANNE: I'm not a baby. Stuart called me a baby!

DAD: Kids . . .

(STUART pokes ANNE again.)

ANNE: And he poked me again!

DAD: OK, that's enough! Stuart, don't poke your sister!

STUART: I was just playing poker. Get it? Poke—her?

ANNE: You're so funny, Stuart. Ha ha.

MOM: We're in the car for another four hours. You two have to learn to get along.

ANNE: This is going to be the longest day in the world.

DAD: Be positive, Annie.

(Everyone is quiet for a minute. Then STUART puts his finger next to ANNE's ear.)

ANNE: Stop it!

(ANNE swats STUART's hand away.)

STUART: Anne hit me!

ANNE: No, I didn't. You were bothering me!

DAD: Anne, don't hit Stuart.

ANNE: I didn't!

MOM: Kids, behave.

(STUART puts his finger next to ANNE's ear again.)

ANNE: Stop it, Stuart.

STUART: Stop what?

ANNE: What you're doing.

STUART: I'm not doing anything.

ANNE: Get your finger away from me.

STUART: I'm not touching you.

ANNE: I'm warning you, Stuart . . .

STUART: I'm not doing anything, Anne . . .

ANNE: Quit it!

(ANNE swats STUART's hand away again.)

STUART: Dad, Anne hit me.

DAD: OK, that's enough. Do you want to go on this vacation or not?

ANNE: Well, not really . . .

DAD: Well, we're going, and you're going to enjoy it and behave back there. Understand?

ANNE/STUART: OK, Dad.

MOM: This is going to be the best vacation of our lives!

Questions

1. Do you like Anne? What is her personality like?

2. Do you like Stuart? What is his personality like?

3. Is Stuart trying to annoy Anne? Is he trying to get her into trouble?

4. Do you think the dad and mom are being fair?

5. Have you ever been on a very long car ride? How does it make you feel?

6. Do you think this will be a fun vacation for this family? What will happen next?

SHOW OFF

Carla got the lead in the school play and now she thinks she is a big star.

Characters

Jim
Carla
Lily
Will
Mr. Hoffman

JIM: I'm glad the school play is over.

CARLA: What are you talking about? I loved the school play.

LILY: Of course you loved it. You were the star.

CARLA: I was, wasn't I? It was so much fun!

WILL: I had to play a camel.

CARLA: I think I'm going to be an actress. My mother says I'm going to be on TV.

JIM: How?

CARLA: Because I'm so pretty.

LILY: You have to be more than just pretty to be on TV.

CARLA: I'm talented, too.

WILL: I'm going to be a garbage man.

LILY: Why?

WILL: I want to jump on and off the back of the truck. And you get to throw garbage.

LILY: Ew.

JIM: I think I want to be a police—

CARLA: Excuse me? We were talking about me being on TV.

LILY: Right. And then Will said he wanted to be a garbage man and Jim said he wanted to be—

CARLA: So what? Who cares what they want to be. I'm going to be famous. All over the world!

JIM: Don't you think you might be getting carried away?

CARLA: Whatever do you mean?

JIM: We just finished the school play a few minutes ago, and you are already planning your Hollywood career.

CARLA: You will be sorry you were mean to me when I'm a big star.

JIM: I'm not being mean to you.

CARLA: You're jealous.

JIM: Of what?

CARLA: Of me! Of my talent.

LILY: You just played an angel in the school play.

CARLA: I played the angel Gabriel! You just played a shepherd.

LILY: I was a good shepherd!

WILL: I was an awesome camel. I even chewed like a camel—watch!

(WILL *chews with his mouth open.*)

CARLA: You guys just do not understand true talent!

JIM: You need to stop bragging.

LILY: Yeah! No one wants to talk to you anymore.

JIM: Your head is so big you can't fit through the door.

CARLA: My talent is so big that there is not enough space in this room for all of us! I'm leaving!

(MR. HOFFMAN *enters.*)

MR. HOFFMAN: Excuse me? I am a talent agent with Star Toppers Talent Agency. I get people jobs as actors.

CARLA: See? I told you guys I'd be on TV!

MR. HOFFMAN: Which one of you is Will Wiggliachi?

WILL: I am.

MR. HOFFMAN: Mr. Wiggliachi, that was the best camel I have ever seen! I want you to be in a movie I'm working on!

WILL: Well, OK. I have to ask my mom first.

MR. HOFFMAN: I'm gonna make you rich, kid. You're going to be a huge star!

CARLA: Whaaaaaat?! Did you see me? I was the angel Gabriel!

MR. HOFFMAN: The angel whosit? Sorry, kid, I don't remember you.

CARLA: But I was the star! My mom says I'm the best actress ever!

MR. HOFFMAN: That's nice, kid. Hey, Mr. Wiggliachi, where's your mom? Let's ask her if you can be in my movie.

WILL: OK.

(WILL and MR. HOFFMAN exit.)

CARLA: This is an outrage!

Questions

1. Do you think other kids like Carla?

2. Do you think Carla will ever be a big star?

3. If Carla got a big acting job on TV, do you think the other actors would enjoy working with her?

4. What do you think Carla's mom is like?

5. If Carla wants to be an actress, what should she do instead of bragging?

6. Which character is most like you? Why?

INSIDE VOICE

Jamie's inside voice is very loud!

Characters

Jamie
Aunt Jane
AJ
Mom

JAMIE: *(Shouting.)* Hey, Mom, what's for dinner?

(AUNT JANE enters.)

AUNT JANE: Your mom had to go out, Jamie. I'm going to make you dinner.

JAMIE: *(Still loud.)* So what's for dinner?

AUNT JANE: I'm right here, Jamie. You don't have to scream.

JAMIE: *(Still loud.)* What's for dinner?

AUNT JANE: Chicken.

JAMIE: *(Still loud.)* Can we have French fries?

AUNT JANE: Why are you yelling? Use your inside voice.

JAMIE: *(Still loud.)* This is my inside voice.

AUNT JANE: Don't be silly. Talk quietly, Jamie.

JAMIE: *(Still loud.)* This is as quiet as I can talk! Can we have French fries?

AUNT JANE: Tell you what, Jamie, if you use your inside voice, we can have French fries.

JAMIE: *(Still loud.)* OK!

AUNT JANE: You're not listening to me!

JAMIE: *(Still loud.)* Yes, I am! You said if I use my inside voice I can get French fries!

AUNT JANE: That's right. And you are still being very, very loud!

JAMIE: *(Still loud.)* I told you, this is my inside voice!

AUNT JANE: And I'm telling you to stop joking around! You're not funny!

(AJ enters.)

AJ: *(Shouting.)* What's for dinner!

JAMIE: *(Still loud.)* Chicken and French fries!

AUNT JANE: Only if you use your inside voice— No, let me change that! Only if you speak quietly.

JAMIE: *(In a quiet voice.)* Why didn't you say so?

AUNT JANE: That's better. Now did you boys do your homework?

(The very loud sound of a train going by is heard while JAMIE says his next line.)

JAMIE: *(Very quietly.)* Not yet. I'll go up to my bedroom and start doing it.

AUNT JANE: What?

(The very loud sound of a train going by is heard while JAMIE says his next line.)

JAMIE: *(Very quietly.)* Not yet. I'll go up to my bedroom and start doing it.

AUNT JANE: I can't hear you.

AJ: *(Whispering.)* I really want some French fries.

AUNT JANE: What?

AJ: *(Shouting.)* I really want some French fries!

AUNT JANE: AJ, you don't need to talk so loud! Did you do your homework?

(The very loud sound of a train going by is heard while AJ says his next line.)

AJ: *(Very quietly.)* I'm almost done.

AUNT JANE: What?

(MOM enters.)

MOM: *(Yelling loudest of all.)* I'm home! Did everyone do their homework?

(The very loud sound of a train going by is heard while JAMIE and AJ say their next lines.)

JAMIE: *(Shouting.)* Not yet!

AJ: *(Shouting.)* Almost!

MOM: *(Shouting.)* OK! I wish we never moved next to the train station!

Questions

1. How do you know when you are being too loud inside?

2. Why can't people just be loud whenever they want to?

3. Which is more frustrating: Not being able to hear someone or having someone talk too loudly to you?

4. Was Jamie trying to annoy Aunt Jane or was it an accident?

5. Would you want to live in this house?

JACK'S GOT THE BLUES

Jack hates music class!

Characters
Lucy
Jack
Ray
Keesha
Mrs. Winthrop

LUCY: Music class—yay!

JACK: Music class—boo!

RAY: You don't like music class?

JACK: I hate music class!

KEESHA: How can you hate music class?

MRS. WINTHROP: Hello, everyone! Good morning. Today we are going to be learning a new song.

JACK: Do we have to?

MRS. WINTHROP: Yes. It's going to be fun!

JACK: What if I don't want to?

MRS. WINTHROP: What's the matter, Jack? Don't you feel well?

JACK: I feel fine.

KEESHA: He doesn't like music class.

MRS. WINTHROP: You don't like music class?

RAY: That's what I said!

JACK: Why is everybody so surprised? Some people don't like math. And I don't like music class.

LUCY: That doesn't make any sense. Music class is fun!

MRS. WINTHROP: What don't you like about music class, Jack?

JACK: It's stupid.

KEESHA: What is stupid about music?!

LUCY: Music is pretty.

RAY: Music rocks!

JACK: I just think it's stupid, OK?

MRS. WINTHROP: No, it's not OK. Even if you don't like music class, you still have to participate with everyone else.

JACK: How come?

MRS. WINTHROP: Do the students who dislike math get to sit out of math class?

JACK: No.

MRS. WINTHROP: Well, then, let's get started—

(*JACK stands up.*)

JACK: But this class is silly!

LUCY: No, it's not!

JACK: It's girl stuff.

RAY: No, it's not!

MRS. WINTHROP: Jack, you have to make a decision. You can stay in music class and do what the rest of the class does, or you can go to the principal's office.

RAY: Sit down, Jack.

KEESHA: Can we learn the new song now?

MRS. WINTHROP: What do you want to do, Jack?

Questions

1. What do you think Jack will do?

2. Is Jack misbehaving or just saying what he thinks?

3. Why do you have to learn things in school that you might not like?

4. Is there a subject in school you don't like?

5. Why do you think Jack says, "But this class is silly!"? Is he embarrassed? Angry?

6. Do you think Jack is good at singing? Do you like the subjects you do best?

IT'S MY PARTY

Zara does not want to share her birthday presents with anyone.

Characters

Zara
Preena
Jackie
Mr. Dobbs

(ZARA sits with toys and wrapping paper all around her.)

ZARA: Thank you, everybody, for my presents! I love them!

PREENA: I'm so glad you like what I gave you!

ZARA: I do!

JACKIE: I love that nail polish Tara gave you.

ZARA: Me, too!

JACKIE: Can I look at it?

ZARA: No.

JACKIE: Why not?

ZARA: I'm going to use it later.

JACKIE: I just want to look at it.

ZARA: You can look at the giraffe Wendy gave me.

PREENA: Maybe we can all try the nail polish on! It will be like we are all princesses.

ZARA: No. I'm the only princess.

PREENA: Why?

ZARA: It's my birthday. That's the rules. When it is your birthday, you get to be the princess and have whatever you want.

JACKIE: Can't you share?

PREENA: You're supposed to share. It's nice.

ZARA: I don't have to be nice on my birthday.

JACKIE: That's not true!

ZARA: Yes, it is!

PREENA: It is her birthday.

JACKIE: But she's not sharing! You're not my friend anymore.

ZARA: I don't care.

JACKIE: I hope my mom comes soon to pick me up.

ZARA: Me, too!

PREENA: Don't fight! Jackie, say you're sorry.

JACKIE: I'm not sorry. I don't want to be friends with someone who can't share.

PREENA: Zara, can you share a little bit with Jackie?

ZARA: Preena, it's my birthday, and I should be able to do whatever I want! It's my present!

(MR. DOBBS enters.)

MR. DOBBS: Girls, what is all this fighting about? Just a few minutes ago you were happy and playing.

JACKIE: Zara won't share her nail polish, Mr. Dobbs.

ZARA: Dad, Jackie wants me to give her my new nail polish, but it's mine! It was a present!

JACKIE: I don't want her to give it to me; I want her to share it with me!

MR. DOBBS: OK, girls, I know a solution to all this.

JACKIE: That she should share?

ZARA: That Jackie should go home?

PREENA: Stop fighting!

MR. DOBBS: No, the solution is that I should get the nail polish.

JACKIE: You want nail polish?

MR. DOBBS: If you girls can't get along, then maybe no one should have it.

ZARA: But, Daddy, it was my present!

MR. DOBBS: Nope, that's it. I don't want to hear any more fighting. You girls play together nicely.

(MR. DOBBS takes the nail polish and leaves the room.)

JACKIE: I can't believe he did that.

ZARA: I'll get it back later. I better get it back!

PREENA: Let's play with something else. Look, you got a game!

ZARA: That's my game. Don't touch it.

JACKIE: This isn't any fun.

(ZARA, PREENA, and JACKIE all sit looking bored.)

Questions

1. Should Zara share? Is she being selfish or honest by not wanting to share?

2. Is Jackie wrong for wanting to use the nail polish Zara just got for her birthday?

3. What do you think should have happened in the scene?

4. Should Preena take Jackie's or Zara's side?

5. Was Mr. Dobbs's solution good or bad?

6. Is Zara right: Can you do whatever you want on your birthday?

7. If you could do whatever you want on your birthday, what would you do?

BABY BLOB

Gus's parents just brought home his new baby sister. Yuck!

Characters

Dad
Gus
Mom

(GUS is watching TV. DAD enters.)

DAD: We're home!

GUS: It's about time.

DAD: That's not very nice to say.

GUS: Mrs. Magee makes meatloaf every night, Dad.

DAD: You like meatloaf!

GUS: Not every night.

DAD: Are you ready to meet your baby sister? Her name is Sheila.

GUS: Sheila? I don't like it.

DAD: You are going to love your baby sister! Here she comes!

(MOM enters, holding a bundle in her arms.)

MOM: *(Quietly.)* Gus! It is so good to see you! I missed you when I was at the hospital!

GUS: Why were you at the hospital?

MOM: Shhh! The baby is sleeping! Gus, I was having your baby sister, of course!

GUS: What took you so long?

MOM: The baby was very small, so we had to stay at the hospital for a few days.

GUS: Mrs. Magee made meatloaf every day.

MOM: Wasn't that nice of her! We really must thank her for taking care of you.

DAD: Gus, do you want to see your new baby sister?

GUS: I guess.

MOM: Come take a look!

(MOM shows GUS the baby.)

GUS: Can she walk?

MOM: No.

GUS: Can she talk?

MOM: No.

GUS: Can she play?

MOM: No.

GUS: Oh.

DAD: Isn't she beautiful?

GUS: She looks all wrinkled up.

DAD: She's beautiful!

MOM: Look at her. She's so sweet. I could just look at her all day.

GUS: She doesn't do anything.

MOM: She will learn to do things. You two are going to have wonderful adventures together.

DAD: You are going to be a very good big brother.

GUS: She's just a baby.

DAD: But she's going to get bigger and faster and smarter.

MOM: You're going to have so much fun! Gus and his little sister, Sheila.

GUS: I hate her.

MOM: Gus, don't say that!

DAD: What do you mean?

GUS: I hate her. She's a girl, and she doesn't do anything.

MOM: You're going to love her. You'll see. Oh! Look! The baby yawned!

(DAD looks at the baby.)

DAD: Oh my goodness! Look at her little face!

MOM: She looks like you, honey.

DAD: I think she has your nose.

GUS: This stinks!

DAD/MOM: Shhhh! The baby is sleeping!

GUS: *(Quietly.)* This double stinks!

Questions

1. Do you think Gus will ever like baby Sheila?

2. Do you like babies?

3. Why does Gus think the baby stinks?

4. Would you rather have an older brother or sister, or a younger brother or sister?

5. Would you rather have brothers or sisters?

6. Do you think the baby will get more attention than Gus?

7. Do you think Gus's parents like the baby better than Gus?

Part 7
CONFUSING!

What are these characters saying?
What's going on in this picture?
You decide!

GRANDMA'S HERE

Mom and Dad said not to let anyone in the house. But Grandma's at the door!

Characters

Joey
Jason
Grandma

(Grandma rings the doorbell.)

JOEY: Doorbell's ringing, Jason!

JASON: I can hear, dummy.

JOEY: Aren't you going to answer it?

JASON: We can't, dummy.

JOEY: Stop calling me dummy!

(Pause.)

JOEY: The doorbell is still ringing! Why can't we go open the door?

JASON: Mom and Dad said we can't. It could be a stranger.

JOEY: What if it's the mailman?

JASON: We can't open the door to anybody.

GRANDMA: Boys? Boys?

JOEY: It's Grandma!

JASON: So?

JOEY: We gotta open the door!

JASON: Mom and Dad said we can't open the door for anyone!

GRANDMA: Joey? Jason? Grandma's here. I'm supposed to baby-sit you. Are you here?

JOEY: Jason, it's Grandma. We know her. We can't let her sit outside.

JASON: We'll be in trouble if we let her in. They told us not to let anyone in! What if it's not Grandma? What if it's a kidnapper?

GRANDMA: Hello? Anybody in there?

JOEY: *(Walking to the door.)* Grandma!

GRANDMA: Joey! Open the door, dear.

JOEY: Jason says we can't.

JASON: Joey, get away from the door!

GRANDMA: Why can't you open the door? It's just me, Grandma.

JOEY: Mom and Dad said we're not allowed to open the door to anyone.

GRANDMA: Well, that's good advice. But you know me. I'm your grandma. So it's OK.

JASON: How do we know you're Grandma?

GRANDMA: You know my voice, don't you?

JASON: You could be pretending.

GRANDMA: But I'm not pretending. I'm your grandma.

JOEY: I think we should let her in, Jason.

JASON: What do you know, Joey? You're just a little kid.

JOEY: I'm almost the same age as you!

GRANDMA: Boys? Look out the window. Then you can see that I'm Grandma.

(JOEY and JASON look out the window.)

JASON: You could be in disguise.

JOEY: Jason, that's Grandma! We could get in trouble if we don't let her in.

JASON: No, we'll get in trouble if we do let her in.

GRANDMA: Jason? I'll prove I'm Grandma. I got you some kind of video game your mom said you wanted for Hanukkah.

JASON: Lots of people get video games.

GRANDMA: And I got Joey the video movie about penguins.

JOEY: That's Grandma! Come on, it's Grandma!

JASON: I don't know about this . . .

JOEY: Let's open the door!

JASON: I don't know what to do!

Questions

1. What should Jason and Joey do?

2. Why is it a good idea not to answer the doorbell when it rings?

3. Will Joey and Jason get in trouble if they open the door?

4. Will Joey and Jason get in trouble if they don't open the door?

5. Do you think Grandma will be mad at them? Why or why not?

YOU'RE IT

When you're playing tag, sometimes it's hard to know who is It!

Characters

Trevor
Julia
Ross

(JULIA runs in. TREVOR runs in after her.)

TREVOR: Tag! You're It!

JULIA: You didn't tag me.

TREVOR: Yes, I did.

JULIA: You just got my shirt.

TREVOR: That's a tag.

JULIA: No, it's not.

(ROSS runs in.)

ROSS: Come on. You're holding up the game!

TREVOR: But I tagged her.

JULIA: No, you didn't.

ROSS: Come on!

TREVOR: Fine. (*Reaches out quickly and tags JULIA.*) Tag! You're it!

JULIA: No fair. You tricked me.

TREVOR: That was fair and square.

JULIA: No, that's cheating.

TREVOR: I didn't cheat.

ROSS: Never mind! I'll be It!

JULIA: No, you're not It. Trevor's still It.

TREVOR: No, I'm not! I tagged you twice.

JULIA: You missed me the first time and you cheated the second time.

ROSS: Come on, let's play!

JULIA: I don't play with cheaters.

TREVOR: I don't play with liars.

(*JULIA and TREVOR sit down.*)

ROSS: Come on, you guys! You can't stop playing. Get up!

TREVOR: She ruined it.

ROSS: Who cares about her? Let's play!

TREVOR: (*Standing.*) OK!

(*JULIA stands up.*)

JULIA: (*Tagging TREVOR.*) You're It!

TREVOR: What?

JULIA: You're It!

(JULIA runs offstage.)

TREVOR: No fair!

ROSS: Come on, Trevor, I'm right here. Tag me! Tag me!

TREVOR: No. I'm not going to tag you if you want to be tagged. *(Runs offstage.)* I'm going to get you, Julia!

ROSS: You guys are so hard to play with. *(Running offstage.)* Why won't anyone tag me?

Questions

1. When Julia says she's not It the first time, is she lying about not being tagged? Being too picky about the rules of the game? Or is she right?

2. Have you ever played tagged with someone who makes up new rules? How does that make you feel?

3. Which character do you like best—Julia, Trevor, or Ross? Why?

4. How do you think Ross feels when Julia and Trevor are arguing?

5. Do you like to tag people who want to be tagged or people who don't want to be tagged? Why?

SMARTY ANTS

Which reading group is the best? Does it matter?

Characters

Rob
MaryJo
Megan
Darcy
Miss Bluebell
Harry

ROB: Which reading group are you in, MaryJo?

MARYJO: I'm in the Smarty Ants.

ROB: Me too! What about you, Megan?

MEGAN: I'm in the Busy Bees.

MARYJO: Oh, that's too bad.

ROB: Sorry.

MEGAN: Why?

MARYJO: The Smarty Ants is the best reading group, the smartest reading group. That's why "smart" is in the name.

MEGAN: How do you know? Maybe the groups are just different.

ROB: They're different because some people are better at reading than others.

MEGAN: I'm good at reading!

MARYJO: No, you're not. At least, you're not the best. You're in the second best group.

MEGAN: Why didn't the teacher say that?

ROB: The teacher doesn't want to hurt your feelings.

MEGAN: I think you're lying.

MARYJO: Ask someone else!

MEGAN: Darcy!

(DARCY enters.)

MEGAN: Darcy, what reading group are you in?

DARCY: The best one. The Smarty Ants.

MEGAN: How do you know it's the best group?

DARCY: The animal starts with the letter A. The second best group starts with a B, the third best group starts with a C. Plus, the word "smart" is in the name of the group.

MARYJO: See, I told you.

ROB: It's OK, Megan. Maybe you'll be in the Smarty Ants next year.

MEGAN: I think you're wrong. If that's true, and the teacher put the word "smart" in the group name because you're the smartest, then how come the C group is called the Clever Cats? Being clever is the same as being smart.

ROB: No, it's not.

DARCY: Being clever is like being able to trick people and figure stuff out, being smart is knowing the most.

MEGAN: I'm going to ask the teacher about this.

MARYJO: Don't be upset, Megan. What reading group you're in doesn't really matter. It just shows who reads better, that's all.

MEGAN: I don't like this at all! I'm in the wrong group! I'm going to talk to the teacher! Miss Bluebell!

(MISS BLUEBELL enters.)

MISS BLUEBELL: Did someone call my name?

MEGAN: I did!

MISS BLUEBELL: What is it, Megan?

MEGAN: Is the Smarty Ants the best, smartest reading group?

MISS BLUEBELL: No, the groups are just different.

MEGAN: How did you decide who goes in what group?

MISS BLUEBELL: It's based on your reading level.

MEGAN: So they are the smartest group?

MARYJO: Told you, Megan.

MISS BLUEBELL: No, no. They just have the most practice doing reading. It doesn't mean that they are smarter.

MEGAN: Oh.

MISS BLUEBELL: Do you understand?

MEGAN: I guess so.

(MISS BLUEBELL exits.)

ROB: So are you still upset?

DARCY: Lots of people are in the Busy Bee group.

(HARRY enters.)

MEGAN: Harry, what reading group are you in?

HARRY: The Daring Dogs.

MEGAN/DARCY/ROB/MARYJO: The Daring Dogs?!

HARRY: Yeah. I totally can't read.

MEGAN: Oh my gosh! I'm so sorry!

HARRY: Who cares. Wanna play tag?

Questions

1. Should Megan feel sad about her reading group?

2. Should Rob, MaryJo, and Darcy be proud of being in the Smarty Ants?

3. Do you think Megan can get better at reading with practice?

4. Do you think it's fair to have different reading groups? Why would a teacher do this?

5. Most people are good at some subjects in school and find other subjects harder. Which subjects are harder for you?

6. Does not being the best at something like reading mean that you're not smart?

7. What do you think Harry is good at?

TIMMY'S STORY

Mrs. Andersen does not like Timmy's story about his Christmas vacation.

Characters

Mrs. Andersen
Timmy
George
Inga

MRS. ANDERSEN: Who would like to read their story?

(TIMMY raises his hand.)

MRS. ANDERSEN: Timmy, why don't you go first?

TIMMY: My Christmas Vacation by Timmy van Horn. On Christmas Eve, I was really excited about Santa coming and getting presents. I wanted a lot of stuff, and I was worried about Santa being able to get it all into the house. I was going to ask my dad about it, but he was busy fighting with Mommy. They were yelling a lot—

MRS. ANDERSEN: Timmy! That's enough! That is not an appropriate story!

TIMMY: What does that mean?

GEORGE: It's not good.

TIMMY: Why isn't my story good?

MRS. ANDERSEN: It's not right to talk about your personal life at school.

TIMMY: My personal life?

MRS. ANDERSEN: Your family.

TIMMY: How am I supposed to write a story about my Christmas vacation without talking about my family?

MRS. ANDERSEN: You're just not supposed to say personal things.

TIMMY: What are personal things?

GEORGE: Bad things.

MRS. ANDERSEN: No, George. Not bad things exactly, just things that are . . . Things that the rest of the class doesn't need to know.

TIMMY: I don't understand.

MRS. ANDERSEN: Let me see. How can I say this? Timmy, you should not have told us that your parents had a fight.

TIMMY: But they did. Mom told Dad to take out the garbage, and Dad said, "I will in a minute," then Mom said, "But there's fish in the garbage"—

MRS. ANDERSEN: Timmy! We don't need to hear these details!

TIMMY: But—Why not? What's so bad?

GEORGE: You're not supposed to tell people your parents fight.

TIMMY: Why not?

GEORGE: You're just not supposed to.

TIMMY: Do your parents fight?

GEORGE: Sometimes. But they don't yell so much. My mom rolls her eyes and my dad says, "That's it!" and he leaves the room—

MRS. ANDERSEN: George! What did I just tell Timmy?

GEORGE: I'm sorry, Mrs. Andersen. He just asked me a question.

MRS. ANDERSEN: Well, let's not talk about this anymore. Let's have someone else read a story about their vacation. Inga?

INGA: This vacation I went to prison to see my Uncle Lou. He stole from people—

MRS. ANDERSEN: OK! That's it! We're not going to read any more stories!

INGA: Can we put our stories up on the wall?

MRS. ANDERSEN: No!

INGA: I like my story. I got a mirror and a doll for Christmas.

MRS. ANDERSEN: Now that's the kind of thing you are supposed to say in your stories.

INGA: I did!

MRS. ANDERSEN: Well, you are not supposed to talk about prison or your parents fighting.

TIMMY: You didn't tell us that!

GEORGE: Mrs. Andersen, can I read my story? There's no fighting or jail.

MRS. ANDERSEN: Very well, George.

GEORGE: I don't have Christmas. My dad says that Christmas is just something companies make up so you buy stuff.

INGA: Your dad doesn't have Christmas?

MRS. ANDERSEN: All right. That's enough. Let's do some math problems!

Questions

1. What is Mrs. Andersen so upset about?

2. Is Mrs. Andersen right to be upset?

3. Did Timmy, Inga, and George do something bad?

4. What does the word "personal" mean?

5. Do you know anyone who doesn't celebrate Christmas? Do you know someone who celebrates another holiday in December? Do you celebrate another holiday in December?

6. What should Timmy, Inga, and George write in their essay?

JOSELYN TAKES OVER THE UNIVERSE

In science class, Joselyn gets caught day-dreaming.

Characters

Mr. Caprio
Eric
David
Pearl
Joselyn
Miss Gilbert

MR. CAPRIO: And those are the names of all the planets. Does anyone have any questions? David?

ERIC: What is the difference between a dwarf planet and a regular planet?

MR. CAPRIO: What is the difference between a dwarf person and a regular person?

DAVID: A regular person is bigger than a dwarf person.

PEARL: Dwarfs are small.

MR. CAPRIO: That's right. So what do you think is the difference between a dwarf planet and a plain old planet? Joselyn?

(JOSELYN is daydreaming.)

MR. CAPRIO: Joselyn!

JOSELYN: What?

MR. CAPRIO: What is the answer to my question?

JOSELYN: I—I—I didn't hear your question.

MR. CAPRIO: Why not?

JOSELYN: I was . . . I was daydreaming.

MR. CAPRIO: Why?

JOSELYN: I don't know. I didn't do it on purpose.

MR. CAPRIO: You daydream quite a lot, Joselyn. You need to listen in class!

JOSELYN: I'm sorry. I didn't mean to.

MR. CAPRIO: Science class is over. It's break time. Everyone go outside and play.

ERIC: Wait, Mr. Caprio! I know the answer to your question. A dwarf planet is smaller than a regular planet.

MR. CAPRIO: That's right, Eric. Outside, everyone!

(MR. CAPRIO exits.)

DAVID: You sure are a space cadet, Joselyn.

JOSELYN: How do you know?

DAVID: What? I mean you keep daydreaming in class.

PEARL: You have to pay attention! You made Mr. Caprio mad.

JOSELYN: I know. He doesn't like me.

ERIC: Did you hear anything in class today?

JOSELYN: Well . . . no.

ERIC: You're gonna be in trouble!

JOSELYN: I know; I know! I just can't help it.

PEARL: What's wrong with you?

JOSELYN: Well, I . . . I don't want to tell everyone.

DAVID: What's the matter? Are you thinking about getting married or something?

JOSELYN: No! That isn't it at all.

DAVID: Then what is it?

JOSELYN: I . . . I think about space.

ERIC: That's what we talk about in class.

JOSELYN: Yeah, but . . . I think about really interesting things.

PEARL: Like what?

JOSELYN: Like going on adventures!

DAVID: You think about space? But you are a girl.

JOSELYN: So?

ERIC: So space is a boy thing.

JOSELYN: It is not!

(MR. CAPRIO enters with MISS GILBERT.)

MR. CAPRIO: Joselyn? May I speak with you?

JOSELYN: Yes, Mr. Caprio.

ERIC: You're in trouble!

MR. CAPRIO: The rest of you should head outside.

PEARL: OK.

(PEARL, DAVID, and ERIC exit.)

MR. CAPRIO: Joselyn, you haven't been paying attention in class.

JOSELYN: I'm sorry.

MR. CAPRIO: Miss Gilbert says that you don't always pay attention in her class, too.

JOSELYN: Well . . . I guess so. I'm sorry.

MISS GILBERT: Joselyn, why aren't you paying attention? It's important to listen in school.

JOSELYN: I know.

MISS GILBERT: Is everything OK? Are you feeling all right?

JOSELYN: Yes.

MR. CAPRIO: Is anything going on at home?

JOSELYN: No.

MISS GILBERT: Then what is it?

JOSELYN: I . . . I think about space. Being an astronaut.

MR. CAPRIO: In class?

JOSELYN: We keep talking about the planets and stars, and planets and stars make me think about being an astronaut and going on adventures.

MISS GILBERT: That makes sense.

MR. CAPRIO: Yes, but you must try extra hard not to daydream in class! It is not acceptable behavior. Do you understand?

JOSELYN: Yes.

MISS GILBERT: If you don't listen, you can't learn, Joselyn.

JOSELYN: I know.

MR. CAPRIO: Now go outside and play.

JOSELYN: Do you hate me, Mr. Caprio?

MR. CAPRIO: Of course not. Now go outside.

JOSELYN: OK.

(JOSELYN exits.)

MISS GILBERT: What are we going to do about that girl?

Questions

1. Do you think Mr. Caprio hates Joselyn? Do you think he is angry with her?

2. Do you think it's fair for Mr. Caprio and Miss Gilbert to be upset with Joselyn for daydreaming?

3. Do you ever daydream in class? Do you do it on purpose or by accident?

4. Do you think Joselyn is learning anything?

5. Do you agree with David and Eric? Is thinking about space a boy thing?

6. How do you think Joselyn feels when Mr. Caprio and Miss Gilbert are talking to her?

7. What do you think happens in Joselyn's daydreams?

ADDY KNOWS THE ANSWER

Addy knows the answer, but Miss Jennifer won't call on her.

Characters

Miss Jennifer
Addy
Jeff
Melinda
Christian
Lydia

MISS JENNIFER: What time is it now?

(ADDY raises her hand.)

ADDY: Oooooo! Oooooooooo!

MISS JENNIFER: Jeff? Do you know what time the clock says now?

JEFF: Ten thirty.

MISS JENNIFER: Very good! Now if I move the hands on the clock, what time is it now?

(ADDY raises her hand.)

ADDY: Ooooo! I know!

MISS JENNIFER: Melinda? Do you know the answer?

MELINDA: Four o'clock?

MISS JENNIFER: No, not quite. That's close.

(ADDY *stands up, waving her hand.*)

ADDY: I know! I know! It's five o'clock!

MISS JENNIFER: Addy, don't speak in class unless I call your name.

(ADDY *sits down, disappointed.*)

MISS JENNIFER: The clock does say five o'clock. But what if I move just the minute hand?

(CHRISTIAN *raises his hand.*)

MISS JENNIFER: Yes, Christian?

CHRISTIAN: Is it five ten?

MISS JENNIFER: Very good! It is now ten minutes past five o'clock on my clock here.

ADDY: I knew that.

MISS JENNIFER: Addy, don't speak unless you raise your hand.

ADDY: But Miss Jennifer, when I raise my hand, you never call on me!

MISS JENNIFER: That is because you make a lot of noise when you raise your hand, and you jump out of your seat.

ADDY: But that's because I know the answer!

MISS JENNIFER: I call on children who are behaving nicely.

ADDY: I can't help it! When I know the answer I get excited!

MISS JENNIFER: I promise that if you behave, I will call on you, Addy.

ADDY: OK.

MISS JENNIFER: One last try. If I move both hands on the clock so they point to the bottom, what time is it then?

(LYDIA raises her hand. ADDY raises her hand.)

MISS JENNIFER: Lydia?

ADDY: You told me if I raised my hand, and I didn't jump out of my seat or make noise, you'd call on me!

LYDIA: I had my hand up first.

ADDY: This is making me very mad!

Questions

1. What do you think will happen next?

2. Do you know anyone like Addy? Do you ever act like Addy?

3. Do you agree with Miss Jennifer's rules?

4. How do you think Addy feels when she knows the answer? How do you think Addy feels when Miss Jennifer doesn't call on her?

5. How do you think the kids around Addy feel when she makes noise and jumps out of her seat?

6. What should Addy do to get Miss Jennifer to call on her?

MOTHER'S DAY

Jerry picked his mother some flowers—from Mrs. Hadwell's front yard!

Characters

Jerry
Mom
Mrs. Hadwell

(JERRY runs into the kitchen carrying flowers. MOM is sitting at the kitchen table.)

JERRY: Mom! Mom! Look what I brought you!

MOM: Jerry! These flowers are beautiful!

JERRY: I picked them for you. Happy Mother's Day!

MOM: That was so nice of you. Thank you for thinking of me.

JERRY: You're the best mom in the world.

MOM: Thank you!

JERRY: You're supposed to give flowers, right?

MOM: You can give me whatever you want.

JERRY: I wanted to give you flowers.

MOM: Flowers are the perfect things to give me.

JERRY: The TV said to give flowers.

MOM: I'm also very happy to get the cup you made me in art class.

JERRY: It's kind of crooked.

MOM: I love it exactly as it is. Do you know why I love it?

JERRY: No.

MOM: Because you made it for me!

(MRS. HADWELL knocks at the door.)

MRS. HADWELL: *(From outside.)* Excuse me! Is anyone home?

(MOM gets up and answers the door with the flowers still in her hand.)

MOM: Oh, hello, Mrs. Hadwell! What can I do for you?

MRS. HADWELL: *(Grouchy.)* You can give me those flowers!

MOM: My son gave me these flowers for Mother's Day!

MRS. HADWELL: Know where he got them?

MOM: Probably the park. Jerry, where did you get these flowers?

MRS. HADWELL: I'll tell you where he got them! He got them from my front yard!

MOM: Oh. Jerry, is this true?

MRS. HADWELL: Of course it's true. I saw it with my own eyes!

MOM: Jerry, is this true?

MRS. HADWELL: Are you deaf? I just told you it was true.

MOM: Excuse me, Mrs. Hadwell. I want to hear the story from my son. Jerry, where did you get these flowers?

JERRY: Well, I . . . I didn't think I did anything bad. There were lots and lots of flowers there, and they were so pretty, and the TV said to give your mother flowers for Mother's Day, and I didn't know they were hers!

MRS. HADWELL: You didn't know they were mine? They were in my front yard!

MOM: Was he being sneaky when he picked your flowers?

MRS. HADWELL: No! That's the worst part! He just went right up and picked them in clear sunlight!

MOM: It sounds to me like he didn't know he was doing anything wrong.

MRS. HADWELL: Maybe so, but now all my flowers are gone! What are you going to do about that?

MOM: *(Handing MRS. HADWELL the flowers in her hand.)* Here. These are your flowers. We are very sorry. Aren't we, Jerry?

JERRY: I didn't know I did anything wrong.

MOM: But now you do. Come apologize to Mrs. Hadwell.

JERRY: Do I have to?

MRS. HADWELL: See? That boy has terrible manners.

MOM: Jerry! You do have to apologize. You picked Mrs. Hadwell's flowers from her front yard.

JERRY: Aren't you supposed to pick flowers?

MRS. HADWELL: No! What do you teach this boy? Flowers are supposed to stay in the ground. I want my flowers to stay in my front yard. Got that, boy?

MOM: Why don't you just say you're sorry to Mrs. Hadwell, Jerry.

JERRY: OK. If I have to. I'm sorry, Mrs. Hadwell. I didn't know they were your flowers. And I didn't know that they were supposed to stay in the ground. But do you have to take them away? They were for my mom!

MRS. HADWELL: These are my flowers, and I'm taking them!

(MRS. HADWELL leaves with the flowers.)

MOM: Jerry, why wouldn't you apologize to Mrs. Hadwell when I asked you to?

JERRY: She's a mean lady. I don't like her. And I'm mad she took those flowers! Those flowers were for you! I hate her.

MOM: Jerry, you don't hate her!

JERRY: Yes, I do!

MOM: I won't have you talking like that, Jerry. Go to your room.

JERRY: But Mom—

MOM: Go on.

(JERRY starts to leave.)

MOM: Wait just a minute.

JERRY: What did I do now?

MOM: Have you ever heard the saying, "It's the thought that counts"?

JERRY: No.

MOM: What do you think it means?

JERRY: I don't know.

MOM: It means that I'm happy just because you wanted to give me flowers. That's enough for me.

JERRY: Does that mean I don't have to go to my
room?

MOM: I still want you to go to your room and
think about how you talked to Mrs. Hadwell.
But thank you for the flowers, Jerry. They were
beautiful.

JERRY: Happy Mother's Day, Mom.

(JERRY exits.)

Questions

1. Why was Mrs. Hadwell angry? Can you understand why she got angry with Jerry?

2. Who spoke more rudely—Jerry or Mrs. Hadwell? Why?

3. Should Mrs. Hadwell have taken the flowers with her?

4. Should Jerry be punished? If so, what should his punishment be?

5. What does "it's the thought that counts" mean? Do you think that this saying is true?

6. Do you feel sorry for Jerry? If so, why?

7. Do you think flowers should be picked or do you think they should stay in the ground?

8. Should you buy or get things because the TV tells you to? Have you ever wanted anything just because you saw it on TV?

9. Which present do you think Jerry's mom liked better—the flowers or the cup he made in art class? Or does she like both presents the same?

POOR BEN

Ben comes to school dirty. Why?

Characters

Daniel
Ben
Adam
Eloise

DANIEL: What happened to you?

BEN: What do you mean?

DANIEL: Your clothes are dirty.

BEN: Nothing. I just . . . fell into some mud on the way to school.

ADAM: That happens to you a lot.

DANIEL: You even have dirt behind your ears!

BEN: I guess I do fall in the mud a lot.

ADAM: How come you're not wet?

BEN: I don't know.

DANIEL: That is weird. You should be wet!

BEN: I guess the mud was kind of dry.

ADAM: Mud can't be dry.

BEN: I don't know. I—I—gotta go.

DANIEL: Where are you going?

BEN: I don't know. I just have to . . . do something.

ADAM: OK, bye.

(ELOISE enters.)

ELOISE: *(Whispering.)* You guys, come over here!

ADAM: What?

ELOISE: You shouldn't have said that stuff to Ben.

ADAM: Why not?

ELOISE: Because . . . you know about Ben.

DANIEL: Know what?

ELOISE: About his life. Don't you know?

ADAM: Know what?

ELOISE: Ben's family is poor. They don't have money.

DANIEL: So?

ELOISE: Soooo, that's the reason why his clothes are dirty.

ADAM: Why didn't he just say that?

ELOISE: He's embarrassed.

ADAM: Why?

DANIEL: Who cares if he's poor? I don't care.

ELOISE: Maybe you don't care, but Ben probably feels bad that he doesn't have nice clothes, and he doesn't get to take a bath all the time.

ADAM: I hate taking baths.

DANIEL: I wish I could not take baths!

ELOISE: But don't you get it? Ben doesn't like being different.

ADAM: Well, Ben's still my friend no matter what.

ELOISE: That's good, but try to think about how he feels.

DANIEL: Should we say we're sorry?

ELOISE: No. Just don't talk about his clothes anymore!

DANIEL: OK.

ADAM: Sure, fine.

DANIEL: I just didn't know.

ADAM: Me either.

ELOISE: Well, now you do. Shhh! Here he comes!

(BEN enters.)

ELOISE: Hi, Ben!

Questions

1. Will Daniel and Adam still play with Ben?

2. Will Daniel and Adam talk about Ben's clothes anymore?

3. How do you think Ben felt when Daniel and Adam were talking about how he looked?

4. Were Daniel and Adam being mean on purpose?

5. What should you do if you notice someone looks different from you?

6. Should Ben be ashamed of being poor? Do you understand why he might feel embarrassed to have less than everyone else around him?

7. What do you think Ben's life is like outside school?

HAPPY FACE

Mom and Dad are fighting, and Bella doesn't want to smile anymore.

Characters
Dad
Mom
Bella
Nate

(MOM and DAD are arguing. BELLA is hiding in the corner.)

DAD: I work all day. All I want to come home to is a clean house and dinner on the table!

MOM: And I would like to have a husband who doesn't yell at me!

DAD: You're impossible!

MOM: You think I do nothing all day long. While you are at work, I cook, I clean, I take care of the kids, I do wash the clothes—

DAD: I'm going to get a pizza.

(DAD leaves. BELLA stands up. MOM sees BELLA.)

MOM: Bella! I didn't know you were in here.

BELLA: I heard you fighting.

MOM: We weren't fighting!

BELLA: It sounded like fighting.

MOM: No, no. Everything is fine.

BELLA: Are you sure?

MOM: Everything is fine, honey.

BELLA: Dad went to get pizza?

MOM: Why don't we eat waffles for dinner? You love waffles.

BELLA: Why don't we have pizza with Dad?

MOM: Oh, he just needs to cool off.

BELLA: Cool off? That means he is mad.

MOM: He will be fine when he comes home.

BELLA: What if he never comes home?

MOM: Daddy will come home. He loves you.

BELLA: Does Daddy love you?

MOM: Yes. We just had a little . . . disagreement.

BELLA: Oh.

MOM: Show me a smile, sweetie.

BELLA: I don't think I want to smile.

MOM: Come on. Show Mommy a smile.

BELLA: Well . . . OK.

(BELLA smiles.)

MOM: Now that's better! You'll see. Daddy's going to come home soon, and everything will be fine.

BELLA: OK.

MOM: Nate! Come down to dinner! We're having waffles.

(NATE runs into the room.)

MOM: How was school today, you two?

BELLA: (Smiles.) It was OK.

MOM: That's great!

NATE: Bella threw up in the lunchroom.

MOM: You did? Why didn't you say so?

BELLA: It doesn't matter.

MOM: Sure, it does.

NATE: Where's Dad?

MOM: He's coming home soon.

NATE: You were fighting again.

MOM: We weren't fighting! Everything is fine. No more sad faces! Let's all smile and go eat some waffles!

(NATE runs out of the room, smiling.)

MOM: Come on, honey, let's go eat!

   (MOM exits, smiling.)

BELLA: Nothing goes right for me.

   (BELLA exits, looking sad.)

MOM: Come on, Bella, smile!

Questions

1. Is it good to pretend to be happy when you are not happy?

2. Is it good to pretend everything is fine when it is not fine?

3. If Bella could tell her mom how she feels, what would she say?

4. Why did Dad leave to get pizza? Do you think Dad is coming back home?

5. Why do people fight? When people fight, does that mean they don't like each other?

6. Is Mom wrong to make Bella smile when she doesn't want to?

7. What can Bella do to be happier?

8. Is it Bella or Nate's fault that their parents are fighting?

9. Do you think Dad and Mom love Nate and Bella?

ABOUT THE AUTHOR

Kristen Dabrowski is an actress, writer, acting teacher, and director. The actor's life has taken her all over the United States and England. Her other books, published by Smith and Kraus, include *My First Monologue Book; 111 Monologues for Middle School Actors; The Ultimate Audition Book for Teens 3, 11,* and *12; 20 Ten-Minute Plays for Teens;* the Teens Speak series; and the educational 10+ play series (six books, including two volumes for kids). Currently, she lives in the world's smallest apartment in New York City. You can contact the author at monologuemadness @yahoo.com.